every day is a journey, and the journey itself is home

—matsuo bashō

*even the briefest form of poetry
can have a wingspan of immeasurable breadth*

—jane hirshfield

How to Write a Form Poem: A Guided Tour of 10 Fabulous Forms

includes anthology & prompts!

sonnets, sestinas, haiku, villanelles, pantoums, ghazals, rondeaux, odes & more + variations

t a n i a   r u n y a n

s a r a   b a r k a t • l . l .   b a r k a t ,   e d i t o r s

FG *field guide series*

ts T. S. Poetry Press • New York

T. S. Poetry Press
Ossining, New York
Tspoetry.com

This book contains references to the following companies, brands, and sources: *Olio*, by Tyehimba Jess, Wave Books, 2016; KitchenAid is a registered trademark of Whirlpool Properties, Inc.; My Little Pony is a registered trademark of Hasbro, Inc.; Frisbee is a registered trademark of Wham-O Holding, Ltd.; *Wingbeats: Exercises & Practice in Poetry*, by Rosa Alcalá, Dos Gatos Press, 2011; *Fair Copy,* by Rebecca Hazelton, Ohio State University Press, 2012; *Odes*, by Sharon Olds, Knopf, 2016; *Newspaper Blackout*, by Austin Kleon, Harper Perennial, 2010; *On the Spectrum: Autism, Faith & the Gifts of Neurodiversity*, by Daniel Bowman, Jr., Brazos Press, 2021; *Haiku: A Poet's Guide*, by Lee Gurga, Charles Trumbull, ed., Modern Haiku Press, 2003; *The Haiku Handbook: How to Write, Share, and Teach Haiku*, by William Higginson, Kodansha USA, 1992.

Cover image by L.L. Barkat.

Cataloging-in-Publication Data:

Runyan, Tania, author
Barkat, Sara; Barkat, L.L., editors
    [Nonfiction/Poetry/Language Arts.]
    How to Write a Form Poem: A Guided Tour of
    10 Fabulous Forms: includes anthology & prompts!—
    sonnets, sestinas, haiku, villanelles, pantoums, ghazals,
    rondeaux, odes & more + variations

ISBN: 978-1-943120-49-9

with gratitude for the back deck
that welcomed me to its solitude
in a time of loss

Contents

Opening Map

Life is short, and you don't need anyone telling you what kind of poem to write. You especially don't need anyone teaching you a complicated formula with which to express yourself. Doesn't that defeat the purpose of "creative" writing? And anyway, it's not like it's 1723. Generations of fore-poets have worked hard to earn us the right to compose in free verse. Walt Whitman shall not have labored in vain!

Still, as Mark Strand and Eavan Boland write, "Forms are—as we believe—not locks, but keys." Forms don't just open doors; they can start a journey and ultimately determine where you land.

Having moved across the country after college, then having three kids (which really racks up the cost of plane tickets!), my husband and I quickly became believers in the road trip. With his job as a high school teacher and mine as a writer, we've had the luxury of carving out large chunks of time to ramble across prairies, mountains, and deserts on our way to visit family in California. We've seen and experienced a lot, from the famous Grand Canyon and Rocky Mountains to the not-so-famous, but no less inspiring, object of my affection featured in my book *How to Write a Poem*—a small, metal Loch Ness Monster statue at a city park in Wyoming. Some destinations are on the itinerary, and some are found on the way, even in a spontaneous moment of taking the nearest exit to grab an ice cream cone.

Throughout this book, I'll rely on the travel metaphor to help you get a sense of how each of the ten forms functions. I'll also share my personal history, experience, and sample "destination" (poem) for each of the forms. That is not to imply that I've mastered these; in many ways I'm still setting out. However, I hope that by reading about my personal experiences, you, too, will feel encouraged to climb lighthouses, visit city murals, and stand in the ocean waves to experience the power of these forms. Mostly, I want you to learn just how freeing form can be.

Each instructional chapter will focus on one of ten forms, then end with an exercise to send you on your way. What's important is to *get writing*, to produce that first villanelle, sestina, or ghazal, to see if you can do it. (Hint: you can.) Once you get writing, you can dip your toes into the additional sample poems and prompts at the end of the book. As you advance, you can then circle back to the "Go the Extra Mile" sections, containing next-level suggestions (you can find these sections, written by Sara Barkat, after the end exercises in virtually every chapter). If your, um, *feet* feel tired, or not yet ready for the hike, remember there is **no need** to go the extra mile!

Most of all, my hope is that by working through these pages, you'll discover that forms are not *formulas*, but rather colorful maps to the unexpected, with an abundance of rivers, bridges, side roads, and sights to explore. Enjoy the journey—and the destination—and remember to pack plenty of snacks.

1

The Villanelle is Coming to Town

For a poem that originated in the gentle, rolling hills of the French countryside five centuries ago, the villanelle can be quite the wild ride.

In just 19 lines, eight of which derive from a pair of repeated, rhyming refrains, the form packs quite the poetic punch. Read this poem aloud, and you'll see what I mean:

Three Six Five Zero

I called up tech and got the voicemail code.
It's taken me this long to find my feet.
Since last we spoke that evening it has snowed.

Fifty-four new messages. Most are old
and blinking into a future months complete.
I contacted tech to get my voicemail code

to hear your voice, not some bozo on the road
the week of Thanksgiving dubbing me his sweet
and breaking up and bleating how it snowed

the Nashville side of Chattanooga and slowed
the beltway to a standstill. The radio said sleet.
The kid in tech sent on my voicemail code.

I blew a night on lightening the system's load,
woke to white enveloping the trees, the street
that's blanked out by my leaving. It had snowed.

Lately others' pasts will turn me cold.
I heard out every message, pressed delete.
I'd happily forget my voice, the mail, its code.
We spoke at last that evening. Then it snowed.

—Conor O'Callaghan

The 19 lines of the villanelle are split into six stanzas. The first five stanzas are *tercets*—that is, they're made up of three lines each. The last stanza is a *quatrain*—it's made up of four lines.

Not only does the villanelle *rhyme*, but it also repeats *whole lines*—alternating the first and last line of the first tercet in all subsequent stanzas—until the quatrain, where it does something a little different. If that sounds complicated, don't worry. It's simpler than it might seem, once you take a closer look.

The villanelle follows the rhyme scheme ABA ABA ABA ABA ABA ABAA.

If you want to keep track of the repeating lines, you can note where they are in each stanza: A^1BA^2, ABA^1, ABA^2, ABA^1, ABA^2, ABA^1A^2.

In "Three Six Five Zero" you can see how the end-words rhyme in this ABA pattern, and how the two repeating lines from the first tercet cycle through, alternating as the final line of each remaining tercet. Then, at last, those first and third lines that have been taking turns meet up in the final quatrain.

Take a look:

I called up tech and got the voicemail **code**. (A^1)
It's taken me this long to find my *feet*. (B)
Since last we spoke that evening it has **snowed**. (A^2)
    [the first stanza ends with line A^2]

Fifty-four new messages. Most are **old**   (A)
and blinking into a future months *complete*. (B)
I contacted tech to get my voicemail **code** (A^1)
    [the second stanza ends with line A^1]

[The third stanza ends with line A^2; the fourth stanza ends with line A^1; the fifth stanza ends with line A^2.]
    Then, the final quatrain goes:

Lately others' pasts will turn me **cold**. (A)
I heard out every message, pressed *delete*. (B)
I'd happily forget my voice, the mail, its **code**. (A^1)
We spoke at last that evening. Then it **snowed**. (A^2)

Whether the villanelle really did spring forth among the grazing sheep of Tuscany is up for debate. According to Amanda French in *Refrain, Again: The Return of the Villanelle*, "The villanelle form has belonged almost entirely to English, and its history in that language dates back only to the late nineteenth century. Moreover, the villanelle has never been so common in any time as it is now."

    Regardless of the villanelle's fuzzy past, its status as a current favorite form is clear. And with today's poets spinning out fresh villanelles every day, its future is looking pretty bright as well.

One of the most recognizable villanelles, Dylan Thomas's "Do Not Go Gentle Into That Good Night," embodies the inescapable pull of death through the cyclical form. The more the poet tells us to fight the end of life with his refrains ("Rage, rage against the dying of the light" and "Do not go gentle into that good night"), the more we can't resist the dying of the light we're told to rage against.

In "Go Gentle," the poet Richard Pierce responds to Thomas with his own villanelle, choosing to play heavily off the "go gentle" refrain, while keeping the middle lines un-rhymed. Throughout this book, we'll talk about variations on forms—how and why they work (or don't) to give shape to a poem's meaning. How does Pierce's villanelle compare to Thomas's, not just in content, but form?

Go Gentle

What good is fighting now? You're dying. Light
will greet you wherever you go. Or it
will not. Go gentle into that good night.

Why rage against your sleep another night
with fists that won't unclench the twisted sheet?
What good is fighting now? Your dying light

shines its blossom of sharpened bones. Your plight,
that silent starving moan of your flickering mouth,
will not go. Gentle into the good night

the moth wings beat the window glass. This sight—
your fear, your fight—destroys us, though none can say it.
What good is fighting now your dying light?

And yet we've gathered as we should. These nights
of final hours. For you, the family, the last.
We'll not go gentle into that good night.

Who knows what the heart will say from that sad height?
Childish, perhaps, I pray, I pray I might:
What good is fighting? Now you're dying. Light
will not. Go gentle into that. Goodnight.

—Richard Pierce

While Pierce's poem is somewhat syncopated, the villanelle more usually takes on a singsong, almost childlike quality. This can be hard to keep fresh, but it can also be turned on its head for disquieting purposes, as in the following poem from Ashley M. Jones.

Her method is somewhat like a game of hot potato: "Kindergarten Villanelle" keeps passing us between two images that should be comforting and safe: blocks and a best friend. In the end, these repeated phrases become a haunting reminder of rejection and injustice.

Kindergarten Villanelle

I'm brown, he's not. The blocks are blue and red.
Jake Jones and I play house every day—

in Kindergarten, it doesn't take much to have a best friend.

I make his supper daily, plastic peas and bread,
we build skyscrapers with our blocks, we play—
I'm brown, he's not. The blocks are blue and red.

We have the same last name, so we wed—
two Joneses are better than one, we say.
In Kindergarten it doesn't take much to have a best friend.

His family comes to visit—it's very unexpected.
I think it is his grandpa, sister or mother—he doesn't say.
I'm brown, he's not. The blocks are blue and red.

They watch us from afar, their faces turning red—
I wonder why they quickly call him away.
In Kindergarten, it doesn't take much to lose a best friend.

The next day, he wants to play with Meagan instead—
her hair is blonde, her eyes are blue. I am cast away.
In Kindergarten, how easy is it to lose a best friend?
I'm brown, they're not. The blocks are blue and red.

—Ashley M. Jones

Take a Ride on a Villanelle

Years ago, our family drove west toward Great Basin National
Park, one of the least-visited parks in the country. The Great
Basin is not a stop on the way to, well, anywhere else. When

you travel to the Great Basin, your trip is all about the Great Basin. And once you arrive at this land of ancient bristlecone pines and the darkest skies in the lower 48, you'll understand that it's worth the drive.

We took US 50, aka The Loneliest Road in America, from Utah to Nevada, where we exited on NV 488 and entered the only town—literally the only town within 40 miles—known as Baker. At the time of our visit in 2012, the town of 65 had no cell phone service. I don't just mean no data. I mean no phone calls, period. There was a hotel, a restaurant, and some stand-alone gas pumps. Not a grocery or convenience store was to be seen.

We landed in Baker during its annual Water Festival, in which the Great Basin Water Network raises funds to counter the Southern Nevada Water Authority's proposal to construct a pipeline from rural eastern Nevada to Las Vegas. It's the little guys against the big guys: dusty carnival rides versus multi-billion dollar hotels wrapped in roller coasters and pyramids.

My kids asked for tickets and climbed aboard rusty little cars attached to spokes. Once the long-haired, leathery ride operator lit another cigarette and flipped a switch, the cars began to rumble.

In a remote place that seemed impossibly far away from everything we knew, the carnival ride gave a sense of immediacy, of now, just like the villanelle. Our long journey was forgotten the moment our kids climbed aboard those whirling cars.

Like a carnival ride, a villanelle circles and spins. At just 19 lines—two of them repeated four times—there is speed, movement, and repeated color. When done well, a villanelle can both exhilarate and disconcert. It's an "in your face" form that wakes you up like a calliope tune, duck-shooting game, or (shudder) clown. It's there, and it's fun, but sometimes it can feel a little too much, like a cycle you can't escape. For this reason the villanelle is a good form for exploring cycles you feel like *you* can't escape. But just like the ride, it's over before you know it.

Every form has its pitfalls, of course, and with the villanelle, the very immediacy and repetition that define it can come across as cloying or cliché. To counter that, draw your readers in with the rhyme and refrain, but also keep them guessing. You can wave at mom during each rotation while simultaneously changing it up: silly one time, dramatic the next, shy another. As with all forms, the structure plays with your expectations by meeting them, and not meeting them, at once.

My Villanelle Journey

What threw me into villanelles was a busy spring of speaking engagements that put me on a number of short flights, some as short as 45 minutes. This proved to be the perfect venue for writing in a fixed form. By giving myself a framework of the villanelle form within the framework of a takeoff and landing, I ventured in the security of knowing that no matter how bumpy the writing journey, I had a good chance of making it to my destination.

Here's one I drafted on a windy night between Milwaukee and Cleveland. There may have been some turbulence, but no spinning, thank goodness.

On the Tarmac

The windsock flutters like a fish
suspended in a hazy bowl.
I close my eyes and vainly wish

that my mind, too, could dip and swish
freely from a steady pole.
The windsock flutters like a fish.

Running late, I dropped a dish,
let it hurtle through the towel.
I closed my eyes and vainly wished

not to be twenty-nine and rich,
but rippling, sunstruck, in my soul.
The windsock flutters like a fish.

The engines roar, the airplane lifts.
I grab the seatback for control,
close my eyes and vainly wish

that my temperament would switch—
ah—to butter melting on a roll
or a windsock fluttering like a fish.
I close my eyes. In vain, I wish.

Flying happened to be a good scenario for me, but you don't
need to go through TSA to draft a villanelle. Get started with
any kind of time framework that's long enough to form the

poem but not so long you let perfectionism stall the important generative process—perhaps around an hour. Revisions can—and oh, they will—come later.

The following situations may be conducive to writing a quick first draft of a villanelle:

> Waiting for a load of laundry to dry
> Waiting for an oil change
> Waiting for school to start after getting dropped off early
> Waiting to be called up at the DMV
> Waiting for a kid's swimming lesson or gymnastics class
> Waiting for the concert doors to open
> Waiting for a pie, banana bread, or lasagna to bake
> Waiting for kids to brush teeth and put on pajamas
> Waiting to reach a destination by car, bus, or train

Notice a theme? We usually think of *waiting* as boring, but writing a villanelle, like visiting a carnival, is a wake-up for the senses. Since it's such a short form that engages in immediate, head-first thinking—more than the winding sestina or detailed ode does—you may find yourself diving into conclusions right away, then making sense of those conclusions later, rather than the other way around. You may find yourself *making* meaning rather than exploring your way into it, which can feel as reckless and strangely whimsical as a carnival in the middle of Nevada.

Your Leg of the Trip

First, a quick recap of how to craft the villanelle form:
• 19 lines—in six stanzas

- First five stanzas are *tercets* (three lines each)
- Last stanza is a *quatrain* (four lines)
- Repeats *whole lines*—alternating the first and last line of the first tercet as the last line in all subsequent stanzas—until the quatrain, which places *both* the first and last line of the first tercet consecutively as its last two lines
- Rhyme scheme: ABA ABA ABA ABA ABA ABAA
- Rhyme scheme with repeating lines noted: A^1BA^2, ABA^1, ABA^2, ABA^1, ABA^2, ABA^1A^2

Ready to take a spin? Here's how:

1. Wherever you're sitting, write a line inspired by anything you see. Don't think too hard. Just record an observation that catches you off guard, troubles you, delights you, or gets you thinking, even if it doesn't necessarily feel "important." Yet.
2. Write a second line that naturally follows from the first. This will set you up for your middle-line rhyme scheme.
3. Before going any further, look up the two end-words you have so far, in a rhyming dictionary or app. Jot down several words for both rhymes. Don't worry that you are "forcing" a rhyme at this point. Think of it as a word bank, which is really an idea bank that will open you to possibilities.
4. At this point, you'll know if you need to switch things around. For example, originally my first line ended in *flutters*. Rhyming with *fish* opens up more possibilities, so I rearranged words. If you're stuck with a word without any rhymes and barely any near-rhymes, like the infa-

mous *orange*, you may want to rewrite that second line.

5. Write the third line in a way that connects, of course, but don't worry too much right now about how or whether this line is going to work in the villanelle as a whole. The structure will lead you.

6. Now that you have your first stanza, write/type the end lines in position on the page (lines 6, 9, 12, 15, 18, 19) so you can see where you'd headed. It helps to see so much of the poem already finished before you start! Of course, you may create some slight variations to these lines, which I think can make for a more interesting villanelle. But having them there really helps as a visual cue.

7. Enjoy the ride of writing those 19 lines. You may be surprised by how quickly you get there!

Notes for the Journey

If this is one of your first form poems, you may initially see the rhyme and structure as too limiting. This is where the imagination comes in. I wrote a second line that ended in *curb* and found myself thinking about *disturb, perturb, verb?* These aren't words I would have thought of before, and that's the beauty. By thinking through the possibilities, I'm seeing my subjects in new ways and uncovering connections and emotions I didn't even know were there. If for some reason I still can't get it to work in a way I like? The worst that can happen is I replace the end-word on the second line or start over with a couple of new lines, with a brain that's been awakened.

Go the Extra Mile (Try Trimeter)

Though villanelles aren't really written in any particular meter, there are several meters in which they've been composed over the years. (One reason many older villanelles can have a singsongy feel is that they used a short meter with a pattern. What was the point of this song-like feel? Well, villanelles, before they became a fixed form with rules about how to write one, were just country songs that people would make up and sing together!)

The most succinct meter that has been used for villanelles is the trimeter. That's a meter with three (*tri*) feet to a line.

You may be familiar with *iambic pentameter* (if not, you can take a peek at the sonnet chapter), and, if so, you might know that "feet" are just syllable combos. For instance, an *iamb* is a foot with the stressed part on the last of the two syllables, like so: da-DUM. A *trochee* is the opposite: the stressed part is on the beginning of the two syllables. DUM-da. (Think of the word *country*.)

So, an iambic trimeter goes: da-DUM da-DUM da-DUM... that's it! That's the whole line!

Meanwhile, in the *trochaic* (trochaic just means "having trochees in it") version of a trimeter, it would simply go: DUM-da DUM-da DUM-da.

Song-like poems aren't in fashion now the way they were in the 19th century, but you can take a spin at one anyhow. If you're not sure whether your tone is working, just ask: if this were a song put to music, would I want to listen to it?

2

The Sonnet Is a Walk in the Park

I bet many of you have written at least one sonnet—maybe during your freshman year of high school when your teacher, bracing for the groans, introduced Shakespeare. You may have rhymed *love* with *dove* and *life* with *strife*. I'm pretty sure I did. No shame there. Writing that first sonnet is about survival.

The centuries-long popularity of the sonnet is no accident. There is something in the rhythm, whether an English/Elizabethan/Shakespearean or Italian/Petrarchan sonnet, that connects to our movement and breath—like a walk in the park.

In this book, I'm going to focus on the Elizabethan sonnet, Shakespeare's trademark form. In fact, because of Will's obsession with the form—he published 154 sonnets, but who knows how many others he wrote?—it's also known as the *Shakespearean sonnet*. The following is a favorite of mine: funny, endearing, and masterful in form:

Sonnet 130

My mistress' eyes are nothing like the sun;
Coral is far more red than her lips' red;
If snow be white, why then her breasts are dun;
If hairs be wires, black wires grow on her head.
I have seen roses damask'd, red and white,
But no such roses see I in her cheeks;

And in some perfumes is there more delight
Than in the breath that from my mistress reeks.
I love to hear her speak, yet well I know
That music hath a far more pleasing sound;
I grant I never saw a goddess go;
My mistress, when she walks, treads on the ground:
And yet, by heaven, I think my love as rare
As any she belied with false compare.

—William Shakespeare

The traditional Shakespearean sonnet has 14 lines: three *quatrains* (four-line stanzas) and one rhyming *couplet* (two-line stanza). It's also written in *iambic pentameter*, meaning each line is comprised of ten syllables with the stress falling on the second syllable of each pair.

The last couplet usually signals a turn, known as the *volta*. (The volta appears before the final six lines in an Italian or Petrarchan sonnet.) In Sonnet 130 above, notice how the speaker, who until now has cataloged details of this not-so-conventionally-beautiful woman, does a bait and switch at line thirteen: "And yet. . ." His cherished love is in fact too rare to be likened to those boring old roses and perfume!

The versatility of the sonnet makes it a timeless form to explore emotions in a brief stroll that takes us to unexpected places. People often worry about how to pull off the turn, but when reading these sonnets, each one from a different century, you get the idea that the change of heart and direction grows out of the form itself.

Bright star, would I were stedfast as thou art

Bright star, would I were stedfast as thou art—
    Not in lone splendour hung aloft the night
And watching, with eternal lids apart,
    Like nature's patient, sleepless Eremite,
The moving waters at their priestlike task
    Of pure ablution round earth's human shores,
Or gazing on the new soft-fallen mask
    Of snow upon the mountains and the moors—
No—yet still stedfast, still unchangeable,
    Pillow'd upon my fair love's ripening breast,
To feel for ever its soft fall and swell,
    Awake for ever in a sweet unrest,
Still, still to hear her tender-taken breath,
And so live ever—or else swoon to death.

—John Keats

I Shall Return

I shall return again; I shall return
To laugh and love and watch with wonder-eyes
At golden noon the forest fires burn,
Wafting their blue-black smoke to sapphire skies.
I shall return to loiter by the streams
That bathe the brown blades of the bending grasses,
And realize once more my thousand dreams
Of waters rushing down the mountain passes.

I shall return to hear the fiddle and fife
Of village dances, dear delicious tunes
That stir the hidden depths of native life,
Stray melodies of dim remembered runes.
I shall return, I shall return again,
To ease my mind of long, long years of pain.

—Claude McKay

It's Not So Hard To Write A Sonnet, Man

It's not so hard to write a sonnet, Man.
Write of a loving couple paired like rhyme.
Let them get old, but not their love, and scan
your lines so that they dance in time,

the lines, I mean, but yes, the lovers, too.
And let them fight. Let them go broke and break
each other down in ways you never knew
that lines and hearts could break. Let each one take

a turn at burning down what they have made
together. Let them make-remake their love.
You may need to revise. Don't be afraid
of amniotic fluid, tears, or blood.

A sonnet's not so hard to write, my friend.
What's hard is loving so love doesn't end.

—Tom Hunley

The Sonnet Stroll

Walking is good for us—physically, emotionally, and poetically. When we walk, we fall into our own pace and rhythm. Iambic pentameter mirrors the regularity of a heartbeat, English speech, or footsteps.

A line of iambic pentameter is simply five iambs: Da-DUM-da-DUM-da-DUM-da-DUM-da-DUM, each "da" a weak, or unstressed syllable, and each "DUM" a strong, or stressed syllable—like your foot striking the ground.

Take a look at the opening line of our Shakespeare sonnet:

My mistress' eyes are nothing like the sun

Do you feel the rhythm?

My MIStress' EYES are NOthing LIKE the SUN

Read it several times, then get up and walk around the room while reciting the line. Chances are it won't take long before your steps fall in line with the rhythm. In fact, many people memorize poems, and even compose their own, while walking, because of this natural body-mind-language connection.

Falling Out of Step: Variations in Iambic Pentameter

When I walk my dog and she suddenly stops then lunges toward a squirrel. Or jerks over to the side to do her business. Or I trip over a stone or root. These are not always pleasant interruptions, but they get my attention because they disrupt the flow of my walk.

Sometimes a poet may stop us in our tracks with a line that strays from the regular, heartbeat-step Da-DUM-da-DUM-da-DUM-da-DUM-da-DUM. How do you know if the variation is "on purpose" or evidence of shaky sonneteering skills? Here's a simple test: are more than half the lines in regular iambic pentameter? If so, you can consider anything outside of the majority a variation. When employed skillfully, a variation that breaks the iambic pentameter spell also wakes the reader to a different tension or idea.

Where do you see exceptions to strict iambic pentameter in the following Shakespeare sonnet? And how might those exceptions enhance the poem's meaning or tone?

Sonnet 116

Let me not to the marriage of true minds
Admit impediments. Love is not love
Which alters when it alteration finds,
Or bends with the remover to remove:
O no; it is an ever-fixed mark,
That looks on tempests, and is never shaken;
It is the star to every wandering bark,
Whose worth's unknown, although his height be taken.
Love's not Time's fool, though rosy lips and cheeks
Within his bending sickle's compass come;
Love alters not with his brief hours and weeks,
But bears it out even to the edge of doom.
If this be error and upon me proved,
I never writ, nor no man ever loved.

—William Shakespeare

My Sonnet Journey

Some people devote their lives to sonnets, the rhythm of iambic pentameter becoming their very footsteps, heartbeats, breath.

I am not one of those people.

Until this year, I'd probably written ten sonnets at most. That may sound like a lot if you're just starting out, but remember, I've been at this poetry thing for decades. The majority of these sonnets were required for my prosody classes in college and grad school. While I've liked some of them okay, I haven't bonded with them. Writer friends have suggested that I loosen up with the form. After all, I could write anything with fourteen lines and call it a sonnet.

But as I've increased my attention to form in recent years, I've learned that limitations are my freedom. Structure is my muse. Instead of pulling back with my sonnetary habits, I considered, maybe I should push forward even more.

Around the time I started working on sonnets, my poet friend Cameron Lawrence suggested I work on a series of epistolary poems. Excited about the idea, but also remembering I had these sonnets to contend with, I decided to combine the two. Epistolary sonnets. Perfect. But written to whom?

Try addressing yourself at certain ages, Cameron wrote. *Okay,* I responded. *How about my prime numbered years?*

It was a great idea. So pretentiously fun. Then, when I literally did the math and wrote down the prime-numbered ages I've lived, I discovered I'd taken on a monumental challenge: 47, 43, 41, 37, 31, 29, 23, 19, 17, 13, 11, 7, 5, 3, 2.

That's fifteen sonnets. Also, what exactly would I say to my 2-year-old self? And how different is 43 from 41?

But adding these limitations has forced me to contend with some memories, images, and meanings I haven't explored in decades, if at all. Much of my memoir writing focuses on my late teens and early twenties because of struggles and changes I experienced during those years. Still, what about the rest of my life? What poems have been hibernating in forgotten selves?

Writing about these periods of my life with the sonnet form—sometimes Shakespearean and sometimes Petrarchan—often in second person, no less, has uncovered and distilled what was most important to me. I experimented with rhymes until the words I needed showed up. And I walked. A lot.

In moments of poetic decision, I may have felt like I was serving the form, but, in reality, the form was serving me. I've written around half of the prime-number epistolary sonnets and will continue until my fifty-first birthday rolls around.

Sonnet for 13

To the one I love, whose cowlicks grew in waves
so that your bangs resembled handlebars
set atop a face you could not save:
salmon glasses, braces, acne scars.
I have a job for you. Grab a mirror
and stare into the deepest, widest pore.
Gaze into the sheen of oil. Draw near
to the hole that opens like a door
to everything you hate about yourself.

then tie a bikini around your cardboard chest
and run into summer's indifferent wealth
where once you hid with the dispossessed.
Be ugly and free in the eucalyptus.
Toss back your hair and call it delicious.

Your Leg of the Trip

First, a quick recap of how to craft the Shakespearean sonnet form:

- 14 lines—written in iambic pentameter
- Rhyme scheme: ABAB CDCD EFEF GG
- A "turn" of thought, or volta, appears in the final couplet

Now, it's time to get moving.

Pauletta Hansel, Cincinnati's poet laureate from 2016-2018, tapped into the natural walking-sonnet connection by creating the Cincinnati Walking Sonnet Project, based on Rosa Alcalá's "A Walking Petrarchan Sonnet."

Hansel's directions are straightforward—in fact, she doesn't even require rhyme or iambic pentameter, though I won't be so freewheeling. Note, however, that since she focuses on the Petrarchan sonnet, she has the walker create a "volta" at the eighth block. For you, that will happen at the twelfth.

Cincinnati Walking Sonnet: The Steps
- 14 lines
- Each line is roughly ten syllables

- Each line does not need to be a complete sentence or phrase: it's okay to carry it over to the next line
- Your first eight lines will be based on the first eight blocks that you walk; one line for each block
- At the end of the eighth block, turn around and go back the same way you came
- Your last six lines will be based on what you notice for each of these six blocks back
- The turn at the end of block eight represents the "volta" in the sonnet form. It gives you the chance to reconsider the blocks you've walked

Walk Your Own Sonnet

Write your own walking sonnet, using Shakespearean structure. If you're writing in a town or neighborhood, use the twelve-block/volta/two-block strategy. If you're on a campus, modify for other visual and spatial cues, such as major buildings. If there's a blizzard or terrible heat wave outside, try the exercise using rooms or walls in your house, stores in a mall, or other markers to direct the content of your lines.

Go the Extra Mile
(Try Petrarchan and Spenserian + Sequence, Crown, and Heroic Crown)

Are you the type who just wants to keep going, when everyone else is ready for a rest stop? Try these variations on a sonnet, and see what appears on your poetic horizon...

Test-drive the **Petrarchan sonnet,** which splits the 14 lines of the sonnet into an octave (the first eight lines) made up of two quatrains with the rhyme scheme ABBAABBA (or AB-BACDDC) and a sestet (the following six lines) with a rhyme scheme CDCDCD or CDECDE.

The volta (turn of thought) appears at the beginning of the sestet, so the octave states the problem of the poem or sets up the action, then the sestet answers and resolves it. The two segments of the Petrarchan sonnet are almost the same length, so you can give the same attention to each piece.

This is a big difference from the Shakespearean sonnet. In the Shakespearean sonnet you still set up the poem in the first quatrain, but it's resolved by the end of the third quatrain. The real "turn" of the poem doesn't appear until the couplet, so instead of creating a full argument against the first part of the poem, you comment on it, tying everything up at the end.

You can also take the **Spenserian sonnet** for a ride. Composed of three interlocking quatrains and one couplet (like the Shakespearean sonnet), it follows the rhyme scheme ABAB BCBC CDCD EE. And, as with the Petrarchan sonnet, the volta appears after the first eight lines (the octave), right as the sestet begins.

Feeling really energetic? Try a **sonnet sequence,** which is a collection of sonnets on the same theme, usually addressed from the poet's character to one particular person or people.

An example of a sonnet sequence is Shakespeare's 154 sonnets, which tell the story of the poet, his complicated love for a "fair youth" (a young man), and a mysterious "dark lady," who all become embroiled in a love triangle.

If you're royally on a roll, you can create a **crown of son-**

nets—a sequence where the sonnets are linked to each other through form: each new sonnet uses the last line of the previous sonnet as its own first line. To end the sequence, the *first line* of the *first sonnet* is repeated as the *last line* of the *last sonnet*.

An example of a crown of sonnets includes "A Crown of Sonnets Dedicated to Love," a fourteen-line segment in the longer sonnet sequence *Pamphilia to Amphilanthus*, by Lady Mary Wroth, published in 1621. The sequence follows Pamphilia's longing for Amphilanthus despite his unfaithfulness.

Finally, if you're feeling super motivated, you can compose a **heroic crown** (or **sonnet redoublé**), which is a crown of sonnets fifteen sonnets long. It follows the same rules as a regular crown—but when it comes to finishing this sequence, the fifteenth sonnet is made up *entirely* of the first lines of the earlier fourteen sonnets, in order. The last, fifteenth sonnet is also known as the "master sonnet."

An example of a heroic crown is *Sonetni venec* written in 1833 by France Prešeren, translated as *A Wreath of Sonnets* or *A Garland of Sonnets*. The master sonnet also contained an acrostic, spelling out Primicovi Julji, ("to Julija Primic"—the woman he was unsuccessfully trying to woo.) It compares the poet's unhappy state with that of his homeland, Slovenia.

Tyehimba Jess writes a complex twist on the heroic crown in his poetry book *Olio,* with sonnets that can be read in any direction on the page.

3

I Sestina the Light

I'm not even going to *try* to be unbiased. I adore sestinas. They're my favorite poetic form, hands down. And they're kinda nuts.

A sestina is a complex French form invented by the troubadour Arnaut Daniel in the 12th century. Usually unrhymed, it is made up of six stanzas of six lines each (a *sixain*), with one last stanza—known as the *envoi*—to wrap it all up, that has only three lines (a *tercet*).

Instead of rhyming, the sestina gets its form from the repetition of end-words (*teleutons*). The six teleutons (we can call them 1 2 3 4 5 and 6) introduced in stanza one reappear at the end of each subsequent stanza, but not in the same order.

Instead, here's the order:

Teleuton (End-Word) Appearances

Stanza one:	1 2 3 4 5 6
Stanza two:	6 1 5 2 4 3
Stanza three:	3 6 4 1 2 5
Stanza four:	5 3 2 6 1 4
Stanza five:	4 5 1 3 6 2
Stanza six:	2 4 6 5 3 1
Envoi:	2–5, 4–3, 6–1

You can always copy from a written diagram like this to track what end-words go where in each stanza, but it can also be nice to know the pattern behind it. That way, if you're on your own, as long as you remember the rule, you can write this block out yourself and compose a sestina anywhere—whether you have this book, or the Internet, or not.

We start with the first stanza. Imagine each of the six lines, with numbers representing their end-words. So far, so good. 1 2 3 4 5 6—the order the end-words appear in first. To get the next stanza's end-word order, use this as a starting point and spiral up, starting from the bottom.

What's the bottom-most word? 6.

You're going up in a conch-like spiral, so the next end-word is going to be the topmost, or 1.

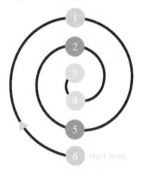

Still spiraling, you go back down to the end-word above 6—that would be 5.

Now take a turn up—second from the top is 2.

Swoop back down—what's above 6 and 5? It's 4.

Lastly turn back up again and end at 3.

So you've now got your end-word order for stanza two: 6 1 5 2 4 3.

To get the end-word order for stanza three, you do the same spiraling pattern using stanza two as your start point.

Stanza Two

6
1
5
2
4
3

Try following the same spiral pattern on stanza two's end-words. Remember to start from the bottom!

What did you get? You should have gotten 3 6 4 1 2 5. This is the end-word order for stanza three.

Now, you might be able to guess how to get the end-word order for stanza four—you just follow the same spiral pattern on stanza three.

Keep spiraling on each previous stanza until you've gotten all six stanzas' worth of end-words written out.

That's it for the six sixains. But what about that envoi? What is 2–5, 4–3, 6–1 all about, anyway? Well, each little dashed group of numbers represents one line; that's why there are three groups. There are two numbers in each group, because in the envoi you're squeezing all six end-words into three lines, which means three of those end-words remain end-words, but three of them get put into the middle of the line. Like so:

Envoi

Line one: 2 is in the middle, 5 is the end-word
Line two: 4 is in the middle, 3 is the end-word
Line three: 6 is in the middle, 1 is the end-word

To figure out the pattern here, you'll have to go back to the first stanza again.

1
2
3
4
5
6

Now, to find the words that should hang out in the middle of your last three lines, start at the second word from the top and hop down counting by twos, skipping a number each time. Notice what you get? 2 4 6.

Then, to find the end-words for your lines, start at the second word from the bottom and hop-skip upward by minus twos, to get 5 3 1.

Put the two lists side-by-side to get your last three lines of:

2-5
4-3
6-1

If you want to play around with the end-word order in the

envoi, go ahead—lots of people do. The most important thing
is that you get the six end-words appearing two to each line.

Got it?

While I haven't memorized the form yet, I declare the sestina my favorite, just the same. This form can be downright
brilliant and haunting. One of the best-loved sestinas from the
last century, and the first one I encountered in college, is this
understated masterpiece written by Elizabeth Bishop...

Sestina

September rain falls on the house.
In the failing light, the old grandmother
sits in the kitchen with the child
beside the Little Marvel Stove,
reading the jokes from the almanac,
laughing and talking to hide her tears.

She thinks that her equinoctial tears
and the rain that beats on the roof of the house
were both foretold by the almanac,
but only known to a grandmother.
The iron kettle sings on the stove.
She cuts some bread and says to the child,

It's time for tea now; but the child
is watching the teakettle's small hard tears
dance like mad on the hot black stove,
the way the rain must dance on the house.
Tidying up, the old grandmother
hangs up the clever almanac

on its string. Birdlike, the almanac
hovers half open above the child,
hovers above the old grandmother
and her teacup full of dark brown tears.
She shivers and says she thinks the house
feels chilly, and puts more wood in the stove.

It was to be, says the Marvel Stove.
I know what I know, says the almanac.
With crayons the child draws a rigid house
and a winding pathway. Then the child
puts in a man with buttons like tears
and shows it proudly to the grandmother.

But secretly, while the grandmother
busies herself about the stove,
the little moons fall down like tears
from between the pages of the almanac
into the flower bed the child
has carefully placed in the front of the house.

Time to plant tears, says the almanac.
The grandmother sings to the marvelous stove
and the child draws another inscrutable house.

—Elizabeth Bishop

When handled creatively, a sestina's repeated end-words don't
bonk you over the head like a cartoon sledgehammer. They
make themselves known in an elegantly obsessive, lyrical manner. How do these words make you feel, just by themselves?

house

grandmother

child

stove

almanac

tears

A sestina's teleutons take on a life and magic of their own apart from the poem. In fact, they are what make the poem magic, and by "magic," I actually mean "real." In an article for *The Chronicle of Higher Education*, Ben Yagoda says this repetition "ineluctably calls to mind the synchronicities and reverberations of life itself."

Read the following sestinas aloud. Yes, as form poems go, they are a bit on the longer side, but what's the rush? Let each poem flow over you, even if you don't "get it" on the first read or two. Just let the words do their work.

Lizards

They're perfect killing machines,
you said to me, dead serious, scheming
something about their silent universe,
the constant shock of their existence.
Despite living your whole life in Florida,
you thought your house impermeable.

In a shoe or on a towel, in your impermeable
mind, they broke up the model-home machine
in which you lived. If you're going to live in Florida

was not something you wanted to hear, scheming
how to stop the arrogant intruders from existing,
how to cast out their soft souls from your universe.

I thought you would air-condition the universe,
caulk the canyons, make the globe impermeable,
throw a tarp over the mountains until all existence
followed your superior plan, ran like a machine.
The lizards took their long pauses, scheming
slow as a hurricane off the east coast of Florida.

This is how your people came to Florida,
you said, refusing to accept a universe
in which one's hopes and schemes
were blown away by the impermeable
will of another tyrant's war machine.
To give in is to betray one's own existence.

This planet has its own existence.
When the storm crawled through Florida,
no shutter, no generator, no machine
could hold up the walls of your small universe.
The house was unroofed, exposed, permeable,
ungirdled as a woman done with scheming.

To you, it was the lizards scheming,
the slow, inevitable pace of their existence
finally amassing enough evil to permeate
your runaway life, your bungalow Florida.
To you, it was personal, this cracked universe,
a failure of your warplan, your inferior machine.

No matter: you started scheming to leave Florida,
to not live out your existence in a flawed universe.
Sometimes one must give in to impermeable machines.

—Celia Lisset Alvarez

The Front Room

There is a grand piano in the corner of the room
where music sheets and magazines pile like a story
on a story, a story of a story, built of stones.
For years, no one had entered that circle
of rug where the corner holds the piano like a flower
closed, or a parasol open against the rain.

But this afternoon it is the rain
that shuts windows, curtains, and house. Room
shrinks to matchbox size. Only a flower
crumbled on the piano top is able to tell a story—
a stem with petals scattered (somehow) in a circle—
while the house hushes as if buried under stones.

Walking toward home I step only on stones.
Balancing my umbrella to stop the rain,
I steal over puddles, sighting the blurred circle
of light ahead which shines from our front room.
The lamps in other windows push each story
into a triangle. Closer, I see window boxes all in flower.

But look! The garden and the world are all a flower
which falls in petals or drops around me like stones
let loose from a cloud's hand in the fairy story
someone always read whenever it would rain.
So now I go into the house and toward the room.
Opening the door the air begins to circle

around chairs, clocks, and tables; the winds circle
in and out of piano legs stirring flower
petals like ashes unsettled in a close room.
The house murmurs, *Open the door. Touch the stones.*
I enter the room. The only rain
of light falls on the stack's topmost story:

"Dollhouses." I turn to page twenty for the story.
Suddenly, the zero of the twenty becomes a circle
which swallows me (like a tunnel) while the sound of rain
grows smaller. I begin to flower
into a child on the page throwing stones
at the house's door, expecting someone to let me into
     the room.

The story outgrows the front room
while rain falls softer than an unopened flower,
and I circle the house, throwing vanishing stones.

—Elise Paschen

To the Lighthouse

As a resident of far northeast Illinois, who travels frequently around Wisconsin, Michigan, Ohio, and Canada, I've spent plenty of time near the Great Lakes over the years. Even though hundreds of lighthouses dot the "Third Coast," I've only admired them from afar until one frozen afternoon in early 2020.

My friend Kristi and I decided to pick one of the coldest days of the year to venture up to North Point Lighthouse in Milwaukee. Built atop a bluff in beautiful Lake Park, the light-house first appeared in 1855, underwent a few rebuilds to keep up with changing needs, and was decommissioned in 1994. Thanks to a number of fundraising efforts, the lighthouse and keepers quarters were restored, and in 2007 North Point opened to the public as a museum.

The 74-foot tower and red-roofed, Queen Anne-style Keeper's Quarters were a welcome sight after Kristi and I spent some time slip-sliding away on the icy path from the parking lot. We paid our $8 admission to a lady with dangling lighthouse earrings who claimed to have filled up three full lighthouse passports with her visits; perused the museum full of a lot of Great Lakes shipwreck information (remind me not to travel back to the 19th century and go on a ship in the Great Lakes); then prepared for our ascent up the 84 steps on the spiral staircase.

Now, I am not a fan of heights. But the process of going up a spiral staircase was so deliberate and controlled (opposed to, say, a glass elevator in a tall building), that I didn't even notice I was quickly reaching the top of a tower.

There is something comforting about looking down on where you've been, one layer at a time. When we say we're "spiraling out of control," we're not quite accurate. A spiral is *in* control. Merriam-Webster puts it this way: "the path of a point in a plane moving around a central point while continuously receding from or approaching it." That seems pretty calm and consistent, if you ask me.

But it's far from dull. While ascending the staircase to the top of the lighthouse, I made several stops to look down and note the curves I had already traveled, surprised at how, in just a few moments, a step I had taken mere breaths ago seemed to belong to a different world while also occupying the space beneath my feet. Climbing a spiral staircase is an exercise in memory, presence, memory, presence—and then you go back down, reliving the experience from a different direction and the perspective of having seen the water's expanse. The steps wind into your consciousness like the sestina's teleutons: never leaving, always changing.

At the top of the lighthouse, Kristi and I took a selfie by the frosty windows looking out over Lake Michigan, where keepers such as Georgia Stebbins repeated the tasks of filling the lantern with oil, cleaning the windows, and checking the mechanism that turned the giant lens. She took those trips up and down the same set of stairs several times a day, every day, each climb and descent with a slightly different temperature and slant of light. She lived out her own sestinas on the lighthouse spiral, the "synchronicities and reverberations" of life pulsing through her patterns of keeping watch.

My Sestina Journey

Back when I wasn't climbing lighthouses, I used to have a habit of snapping off my split ends, zoning out and picking at my hair, at the expense of writing, sleeping, or talking to my kids.

Months of incentives and redirection didn't help. In order to reclaim my time and focus, I had to take drastic measures to remove the temptation altogether. I had to cut my hair short.

With no accessible hair to fuss over and no major worries at the time, my brain found itself looking for a place to go. It needed walls to bounce off, something to obsess over. My sestina-writing project came at the perfect juncture.

Over the course of a few weeks, I wrote, appropriately, six sestinas. Without a doubt, the poems gave my brain a place to go. My anxious synapses latched onto the spiraling pattern like barnacles on a sea turtle.

I approached writing sestinas using various methods to see how the tone and process would change. When approaching sestinas, it's all about the end-words. How will the poet access those six teleutons that will determine the shape and life of the poem?

Here were my various approaches:

1. Use six words that have been on my mind lately.
2. Write a six-line first stanza first, then use those end-words for the rest of the poem.
3. Write the end, or envoi, first, and take the end-words from there.
4. Use six randomly-generated words. I got mine from an

educational site: http://creativitygames.net/random-word-generator/randomwords/6

5. Use six words assigned by a friend.

For my sixth sestina, I repeated #1, using whatever words had crept into my consciousness over the past few weeks.

Each method brought its own challenges (with #1, overall, being the easiest to write and #4 being the hardest). The result, however, was always the same: perseverating over a group of words: how they link in my life and consciousness, how they speak to one another in my heart, and how they tell a story simply by being thrown together, like strangers on an elevator.

Coming back to the same words seven times per poem, like circling those lighthouse steps, forced me to make them work, finding meaning and purpose in their often irritating presence: *You again? Already?* But moving within and around these teleutons helped me see some light; it also helped me shine it out to my readers.

Here's the sestina that came from strategy #5, words assigned by friends:

Seventh Grade Sestina

What's wrong with people? Why's it so hard
to be nice? my daughter wails, the same old
question that's niggled and bruised
humankind spreading like mushroom
spores in her spirit, leaving her in certain
defeat. It seems it should be easy, at first blush,

to say, *I'm sorry; I was wrong,* and blush
into that squashy humility that soothes a hard-
edged world. After school, she was certain
the messages would be forgotten, the old
friendships saved from a mushroom
cloud of degenerating Snaps. But the bruising

words and smirking emoticons continued, bruises
that can't be concealed with foundation and blush.
The original offense: one girl peeled a mushroom
from her pizza and flicked it, hard,
at my daughter's face. Only 12 years old,
and she's translating fungi in flight, uncertain

if it's love or attention-seeking or certain
loathing that's sending a bruise-
colored chip of slime across the old
cafeteria table. Then some girls blushing
in anger and others laughing, *how hard
is it to take a joke? No mushroom's*

ever killed anyone! Then they mushroomed
into teams online: for, against, or uncertain
whether the thrower needed to do hard
time in seventh grade society. Pain brews
beneath the silliest acts. *You would blush
if I explained the stupid things I did from old*

hurts, I told my daughter, *and I'm 45 years old.*
We invented theories about the mushroom

girl: Was she embarrassed for wearing too much blusher?
Did she drop a mini-pad in front of a certain
green-eyed boy? Was her ego bruised
by that algebra test she didn't think would be hard?

By the time the sky blushes with sunset, it's old
news. My daughter's posted a selfie with a mushroom,
and, I'm certain, healed some (but not all) of the bruises.

Your Leg of the Trip

First, a (not-so-quick) recap of how to craft the sestina form:

- 39 lines—six stanzas, six lines each (a sixain), plus one last stanza of three lines (a *tercet*)
- Final stanza is called the *envoi*
- Repeats end-words. The end-words introduced at the close of each line in stanza one reappear at the close of each line of each subsequent stanza, in a new order
- The order of the six end-words for any sixain can be figured out from looking at its previous stanza. The new order will start with the bottom end-word, jump to the top end-word, and continue to move to the vertical center (the second end-word from the bottom, then the second end-word from the top, then the third end-word from the bottom, then the third end-word from the top)
- In the three-line envoi, all original end-words appear. Three still function as end-words, and three hang out in the middle of the lines
- To figure out the placement for the words in the middle

of the envoi, go back to the word order of the first stanza (1 2 3 4 5 6), start on the second line, and hop down the stanza by twos to get three words (2 4 6). To figure out the placement for the envoi's end-words, start at the second line from the bottom and hop up the stanza by twos to get three words (5 3 1) and then put your work together:

Line one: 2 is in the middle, 5 is the end-word
Line two: 4 is in the middle, 3 is the end-word
Line three: 6 is in the middle, 1 is the end-word

Try writing sestinas using a variety of approaches, to see how different sets of teleutons lead you to unexpected places…or, in some cases, how different ideas and lines lead you to unexpected teleutons. While I recommend reading all your poems aloud as you work through your drafts, I especially want you to listen to your sestinas to hear how your teleutons weave emotion and meaning.

1. Use six words that have been on your mind lately. They could be a combination of objects, obsessions, and emotions; colors, sounds, or tastes you've been especially drawn to; actions you've taken or wanted to take. Not sure what those words might be? Look over your journals or social media posts, or ask someone close to you what you've been talking about lately.

2. Write a six-line first stanza first, then use those end-words for the rest of the poem. Don't even think about the teleutons; just begin a poem and see where the first six lines take you. However, do keep line breaks in

mind. You wouldn't want to break at flat articles, conjunctions or prepositions (*the, and, at*) even in a free verse poem; in the case of a sestina, these teleutons would spell *b-o-r-i-n-g!*

3. Write the end, or envoi, first, and take the end-words––two from each line—from there. Yes, that's three stellar lines that sound like an ending, even if you don't know (yet) how you're going to get there!

4. Use six randomly-generated words for your teleutons. Try the educational site I used, or go low-tech, grab a book, close your eyes, and let your fingers land on six words, one at a time. No fudging! : http://creativity games.net/random-word-generator/randomwords/6

5. Use six words assigned by a friend. Be careful of the friend you choose.

Go the Extra Mile (Try Hendecasyllables)

Sestinas not complicated enough yet? Want to add more pizzazz? Try some extra bells and whistles, and write a sestina using the meter established by Petrarch and Dante: **hendecasyllables.**

What are hendecasyllables? They comprise a meter that always stresses **at least** the tenth syllable (*dec!*) and either the *fourth* or *sixth* syllable of the line. Hendecasyllable lines can be ten syllables, eleven syllables, or even twelve syllables long.

There are many hendecasyllabic variations, because even though you need the fourth or sixth, plus the tenth syllable stressed, you can also add even more stresses if you like.

For instance, iambic pentameter, lines of ten syllables

where each "even" syllable is stressed: da-DUM da-DUM da-DUM da-DUM da-DUM is an example of a hendecasyllabic line. Notice that it has a stress on syllable four and syllable ten? Yes, it also has *more* stresses than that, but the necessary hendecasyllabic part's been covered too!

da-DUM da-DUM da-DUM da-DUM da-DUM
1   2   3 (4)   5   6   7   8   9 (10)

For example, these three lines from Sir Philip Sydney's sestina "Since Wailing is a Bud of Causeful Sorrow" are hendecasyllabic. They have stresses on both the sixth and the tenth syllables (see gray text), in addition to stresses on other syllables (see bold text).

Since wailing is a bud of causeful **sorr**ow,
Since sorrow is the follower of ill **for**tune,
Since no ill fortune equals public **dam**age,

Have fun, play around, and see what kind of mileage you get!

4

An Acrostic Over Troubled Waters

It's a classic beginning-of-the-school-year activity: create an acrostic that describes you. First, you stack the letters of your name from top to bottom. This forms the basis of what you'll do next: choose words that show off who you are, each word starting with a letter in your name.

Exhibit A:

Terrific
Amiable
Nature-loving
Intelligent
Adorable

Cute, right? And back in my day, we would probably cut out magazine pictures, too—that would somehow capture our inner soul—and slap those suckers on with rubber cement.

Acrostics have always had a reputation for being fun and easy to write (unless your name is Bartholomew, I guess), and although they can make for a good September icebreaker assignment, they're often not taken very seriously.

But acrostics that do what acrostics are *supposed* to do? They don't mess around. For this reason, they're sometimes used stealthily in subversive public statements—to powerful or witty effect. The statement may be quiet, but it's anything but timid.

Here's an example of an acrostic being its subversive acrostic self. If you want to see the secret more quickly, take a moment to circle the first letter of each line before you read. (Note that poems with extra long lines like this one from O'Hara will "wrap" down to an indented line. When space allows, such poems do not wrap. You'll also encounter other instances of long-lined poems later in this book.)

You Are Gorgeous and I am Coming

Vaguely I hear the purple roar of the torn-down Third
    Avenue El
it sways slightly but firmly like a hand or a golden-downed
    thigh
normally I don't think of sounds as colored unless I'm
    feeling corrupt
concrete Rimbaud obscurity of emotion which is simple
    and very definite
even lasting, yes it may be that dark and purifying wave,
    the death of boredom
nearing the heights themselves may destroy you in the
    pure air
to be further complicated, confused, empty but refilling,
    exposed to light

With the past falling away as an acceleration of nerves
    thundering and shaking
aims its aggregating force like the Métro towards a realm
    of encircling travel
rending the sound of adventure and becoming ultimately

local and intimate
repeating the phrases of an old romance which is con-
      stantly renewed by the
endless originality of human loss the air the stumbling
      quiet of breathing
newly the heavens' stars all out we are all for the captured
      time of our being

—Frank O'Hara

There was a reason O'Hara chose to both show and hide the
name of his partner, Vincent Warren, in an acrostic. He wrote
a number of love poems to Vincent, but "many of these
poems do not mention O'Hara's lover by name, thanks to
Warren's fear that his mother would read them and discover he
was secretly gay." The acrostic, then, is a risk here, but that's
what makes it playful, exciting, and a bit on the edge. I believe
a good acrostic should walk that line. Choose risk over cute-
ness.

Here's another sample of an acrostic that speaks the un-
spoken:

KitchenAid Epicurean Stand Mixer

Another year has passed and she never thought she'd
Get to thirty-three years without one.
One day, when she was seven,
On the kitchen table stood a chrome KitchenAid.
Daring to put forth a vision, blended with
Hearth, she promised herself that,

On that special day of white cakes stacked to sky,
Under a crescent moon with her man,
Slung in his arms, gliding to band tunes,
Emptying her heart to pour in his ambitions,
Welcoming gifts from relatives she somewhat knew,
In her arms, she would have a KitchenAid,
Full of features and heavy-duty processing capability,
Easy to assemble with a double whisk attachment,
Head tilting back so it's easy to
Add ingredients and scrape down the sides of the bowl,
Sensors maintain a constant speed regardless of load,
And a soft-start feature reduces spattering.
KitchenAids still line the shelves at Williams-Sonoma
In military formations on her thirty-third birthday.
Their smooth bodies feel like butterfat,
Curves covered with enamel, boasting form and function.
Her eyes meet the hunter green one in the middle,
Everything she's wanted in life in this box,
Never imagined she would not be married by now,
And still living with a roommate in a flat,
Intimate with a new man every eight months,
Dancing in circles, spinning around and around.

—Victoria Chang

The fact that the poem is "about" a KitchenAid® mixer is no secret. But how does the spoken-unspoken "A Good Housewife Has a KitchenAid" work itself into the poem, into the speaker's persona? (Hint: do an Internet search for KitchenAid ads from the 1950s).

More importantly, how does it work itself into you, the reader?

Don't Look Down! (High Suspense!)

I don't love heights, and the problem with most bridges is they tend to be high. My fear isn't paralyzing enough to keep me from crossing, but, unless I'm the one driving, I pretty much close my eyes until we're on the other side. My memory of passing over the Golden Gate bridge in heavy traffic several decades ago still makes me sweat.

A footbridge over a river may not take as long to cross as the Golden Gate, but it feels truly exposed. Last summer, I went with my family to Pukaskwa National Park on Lake Superior in northern Ontario, Canada. It's a gorgeous park full of natural beauty and history and, wouldn't you know, a suspension footbridge over a river.

The White River Suspension Bridge is the swaying, mist-covered star of an 18-km day trip that winds through wetlands and boreal forests. Unlike some of those rickety bridges you might see on an adventure travel show, the White River Suspension Bridge is made of metal with sturdy-looking hardware and chain-link fencing that should hold you fairly securely 23 meters above Chigamiwinigum Falls.

Still, it doesn't *seem* natural to be standing over a waterfall, so all the protective features in the world didn't help me feel secure when my husband and three kids jumped as hard as they could to make the bridge jostle and sway, causing me to grab onto the sides and turn as white as the water. Much to their delight.

When they tired of torturing me, I was able to stand still for a few minutes and look over the edge. I wasn't at my most calm and comfortable—lying on the couch under a weighted blanket—but I was awake and alive. The churning water reminded me that living on the edge or, rather, a bridge, gives me a more active role in the tenuousness of life. I'm still a spectator of the waterfall. I'm not rafting down it. But walking across the waterfall brings me into its misty grip as I consider it from a different perspective.

I think of an acrostic as a bridge that takes you across a poem, one letter (or step, or board) at a time. Whatever those initial words spell isn't hidden, just as the bridge wasn't hidden from my view on the hike. But once I stepped on, it helped me see and understand the water anew. The KitchenAid poem, for example, works on the surface as a poem about a woman disillusioned with how her life has strayed from expectations. The phrase, though, carries us through the poem with even deeper levels of culture and gender playing into the speaker's mourning.

An acrostic should do the job, but it shouldn't be easy. It can easily fall into gimmick. A little discomfort, a little mystery, is part of the excitement. Cross the bridge with a bit of swaying, and enjoy that sensation. Perhaps even look down when you're not supposed to. A good acrostic, like a good bridge, won't break apart, but it will provide a sense of adventure, a feeling of the bridging work being done.

My Acrostic Journey

Because my friends and I know how to have a good time, one

day my pal Brad and I brainstormed a list of phrases that make us anxious, particularly when we receive them over a text or Facebook message. It may seem like a better idea to just block those from mind rather than writing them down. But there's something about facing danger head on…right? Like walking over a waterfall?

Here are a few of our stomach-clenching winners:

call me back asap
we need to talk
where do I begin
no one's hurt but
message can't be sent
have you seen the latest tweet?

These phrases have in common *the unknown:* what horrible news will befall me? What new relational nightmare is waiting around the corner? Have I been blocked? Usually worse than the news itself is the five minutes, hours, or days you have to wait to find out. It's about lack of control.

The acrostic is a way to take language under control, so I've started writing them, using our clench phrases to explore entrenched anxieties. The form has helped me understand myself, my emotions, and my reactions, by seeing how they present themselves in and through the "restriction" of the letters starting each line. In the poem below, I guarantee I would have never used the words *eke* or *keening,* for example, but wow, do they ring true. The acrostic form challenges us to delve deeper into a word, phrase, title, or name in unexpected ways.

However, poetry is about craft as well as feelings. Journal to your heart's content, but when it comes time to turn your expressions into a work art, that's where your creative and intellectual synapses must fire together, most likely for several drafts. It's simply not enough to just start each line with the letter. It's not an excuse for ineffective line breaks, forced or obscure meanings, or wacky sentences that leave your reader saying, "It's an acrostic, sure, but is it first and foremost a good poem?"

I'm not sure how you'd judge the poem below, but hey: I tried. And if you send me a message saying we need to set up a time to discuss, you might find me curled in a fetal position.

From the Anxiety Series

Whatever this is about, I'm sure it's humiliating,
Even paralyzing because

Never have I forgiven myself for disappointing someone
Else. Grieve me instead, please.
Eke out a reason to offend me and I will
Drench you with understanding.

To be in pain is easier than having caused it
Or, worse, waiting for the conversation

That for now has stopped time
And told my stomach that danger
Lurks in the hours ahead, as I reply and wait,
Keening for your love again.

Your Leg of the Trip

First, a quick recap of how to craft the acrostic form:

- Choose a word or phrase—possibly one that contains a secret idea
- Write the word or phrase vertically down the page, so you have one letter beginning each line
- Use the letters to start the first word of each line
- Complete each line in a way that supports or subverts the message of the word or statement you began with

Okay, now for your leg of the trip.

What do you have to hide…but not really? Is there something you want to shout from the rooftops some days, but whisper under your breath the next?

Using one of the prompts below, write an acrostic. While any close reader will pick up on the form eventually, don't rely on the form alone to drive the poem. It should stand as a good poem that makes sense even if the acrostic slips under the radar.

1. Write a poem to a person, using their name as the acrostic. Unlike the elementary school assignment, the name here should be a little bit of a secret. It could be a lost or unrequited love, a distant relative, someone who hurt you, or someone you are just now realizing has helped shape your life.

2. Honor one of your favorite poems by using a line as an acrostic. See where the letters take you in a way that sheds meaning on the line. As Emily Dickinson says,

"tell it slant." Speaking of Dickinson, the poet Rebecca Hazelton wrote an entire collection of poems that are acrostics from Dickinson lines.

3. State an opinion that could be controversial and make that your acrostic. It doesn't have to be an explosive, political topic. In fact, something like "Avocados Are Gross" (one of my own unpopular opinions) could make for an interesting journey.

4. Take a famous quote, advertising slogan, or popular saying, and turn it on its head, plumb its depths, and/or argue with it using an acrostic.

Go the Extra Mile (Try a Double Acrostic)

Get your alphabet on, and try a double acrostic. In the double acrostic, you make *both* the beginning-of-the-line letters *and* the end-of-the-line letters speak your message. The initial letters are called the *acrostich*, the final letters the *telestich*.

Really beautiful bridge to cut
over the winding river—
all that I
dream…traverses your hip

—L.L. Barkat

(Bold letters in the poem above are for instructional purposes.)

5

Ghazals: A Different Train of Thought

The ghazal (pronounced **zhuh**-zhuhl—with the stress on the first syllable) is unlike any form you've probably written before. Mastering it is not about learning a pattern or technique as much as adopting a mindset. Yes, there are "rules," but the rules alone won't help the ghazal click for you—at least in my experience. By setting aside your expectations about how or why a poem works, you'll open yourself to the mind-and-spirit-shifting possibilities of a form that Hashmi has noted "ceaselessly hungers for the absent beloved."

A ghazal is a form of Arabic verse that goes all the way back to the 7th or 8th centuries. It gained popularity among Persian poets in the 13th and 14th centuries but was introduced into English language poetry fairly recently—around the 1960s.

Ghazals tend to focus on themes of separation, loss and longing, or unrequited love, but their sentiments lean more toward melancholy than bleakness or bitterness. Composed using a series of five or more couplets, certain parts of the poem repeat as a refrain.

Why a refrain? Well, like the villanelle, ghazals have a deep connection to music. In fact, historically, and even now, they're often performed not by being read, but by being sung. Though the couplets don't always have continuity between them, the poem is held together with the same feeling or tone throughout that builds on itself as you read (or listen).

Let's look at the nuts and bolts. Here's a ghazal written by Joshua Gage:

In the Summer

Desperate bodies seek sun in the Summer,
cancerous tans overdone in the Summer.

Though waiting for angels with wings of stained glass,
no visions will come to the nuns in the Summer.

He looks for escape from heat's rabid madness.
His search is futile, there're none in the Summer.

Numb from the neck up, youth seeks elevation
with poison soaked flesh for fun in the Summer.

Her neck punctuated with tendrils escaped,
she woos with her hair in a bun in the Summer.

Chasing the night as it melts into dawn,
the Pilgrim must stay on the run in the Summer.

—Joshua Gage

The basic ghazal ingredients are as follows:

1. Minimum of five stanzas.
2. Each stanza includes two lines, making a couplet.
3. Each couplet should be able to stand alone, as if it were

its own poem. In some ways, this is good news because you don't have to be responsible for creating a narrative. But this is also the hardest "rule" for Western poets to grasp. We'll talk more about this later.

4. Every line is traditionally the same length and follows a consistent metrical pattern.

5. The first couplet is known as the *matla*, and it ends with the same end-word or phrase (*radif*) on each line:

> Desperate bodies seek sun **in the Summer,**
> cancerous tans overdone **in the Summer.**

6. The matla also introduces a rhyme (*qafia*) **inside** the lines, right before the radif.

> Desperate bodies seek **sun** in the Summer,
> cancerous tans over**done** in the Summer.

Notice that this is the poem's *first* couplet (the matla) so both lines end with the radif—*in the Summer*. The qafia, or rhyme, falls right before the radif: *sun* rhymes with *done*.

7. The radif will now repeat at the end of every second line of the rest of the couplets.

> Though waiting for angels with wings of stained glass,
> no visions will come to the nuns **in the Summer.**

Note that *in the Summer* is at the end of the second line. See the rhyming word right before it? *Nuns* rhymes with *sun* and *done*, the qafia first introduced at the beginning of the poem.

8. Ghazals end with the poet inserting his or her name or other reference to the self. This moment of self-reference is sometimes humorous or odd. In this case, the poet refers to himself as a "Pilgrim" who must escape the summer.

Chasing the night as it melts into dawn,
the **Pilgrim** must stay on the run in the Summer.

Let's return back to number 3, or each stanza standing alone. Agha Shahid Ali, in his introduction to *Ravishing Disunities*, describes this important characteristic:

> The ghazal is made up of couplets, each autonomous, thematically and emotionally complete in itself. One couplet may be comic, another tragic, another romantic, another religious, another political...A couplet may be quoted by itself without in any way violating a context—there is no context, as such. One should at any time be able to pluck a couplet like a stone from a necklace, and it should continue to shine in that vivid isolation, though it would have a different lustre among and with the other stones.

The unity, then, comes from the technical consistency, not the content, which Ali calls a "stringently formal disunity."

Of course, the radif (ending word or phrase) on its own brings a sense of unity that can sometimes spill into content. When you're using the phrase *in the Summer,* for example, you're going to be talking about summer. However, as the sample poem shows, there is not a linear story or message about summer. Each couplet does express a longing, or "ceaseless hunger for the absent beloved," which isn't always a romantic interest. What does the Pilgrim long for in this ghazal?

Here are more ghazals to savor. Read them aloud, slowly, opening yourself to the beauty of the language and the echoes of longing. Then experiment by reading the ghazals again, this time switching the order of couplets as you read to see if, and how, the necklace shines in the same way.

Time Falling

God's ear turns to Earth to eavesdrop:
A single bite rings out—Eve's drop.

This one-ring circus, tilted and spinning,
Two hands slip off the trapeze—drop.

One heart shatters, a ball does the same,
A lifetime of New Year's Eves drop.

Proudly we stand, but penitent fall;
As we grow older, all knees drop.

Whose is this face? Whose gray, shedding hair?
Water beads from the window eaves drop.

The face in the window belongs to the wife.
With eyes closed, she sees the last leaves drop.

—Katie Manning

(Note: long-line poem below wraps to indents)

November Pyres

Under currents we first live—before pulse and child
    breathing.
The smallest seed, the mustard grain, the wild shape of
    being.

I knew you once, before burning to air, before charred
    scent.
Adorned with best guess, I dressed in the mild faith of
    being.

Under an Ozark moon, maple fires flamed in November.
It burned through—spirit, marrow—to defiled taint of
    being.

We were phoenixes maybe? Nests and necks all ashen gray?
Rising maybe—the inspired reincarnate of being?

Naught were we though, but two separate pyres, smoking,
    dying.
It, a prying—love from faith, from beguiled shape of
    being.

—Seth Haines

The Ghazal's Station in Life

Years ago, when I worked in downtown Chicago at a publishing company, I took the Metra train from my suburb to Union Station every weekday. This was before smartphones, so I would do crazy things like read books, write in a journal, or doze off for forty minutes.

Like Ali's metaphor of jewels in a necklace, a train route is made up of many stops to constitute the whole. However, each stop also exists on its own. While they link together to serve a purpose, they also have separate identities as individual stops with their own zip codes, people, and personalities.

I remember leaving my station in Northbrook and heading into Glenview, where the same guy with an apple in one hand and a briefcase in the other ran wildly from the parking lot to catch the train on time every morning. Then we'd arrive at Golf, a quiet station with green trim and a brick chimney, Morton Grove with its super-pierced art student smoking around the corner of the shelter, and so on. I memorized the order of stations, the regulars who shuffled on and off each morning, and the conductor's speech patterns. "Heallly, this is Healy," he'd say when we approached one of the last stations before the final stop.

Each station offered its own colors and images. But taken together, they transported me to something even greater: the middle of a bustling skyline. (Unlike the couplets of a ghazal, however, the stations must stay in a particular order—at least until some pretty cool teleporting is invented.)

How does riding the train connect to the ghazal's ever-important theme of longing? Trains have always held some kind of romance. Perhaps it's the rhythm of the tracks reverberating in your bones as you get closer and closer to your destination. Or the distant bellowing of the horn in the fog. Or the long history of those trusty engines patiently hurtling us toward the jobs we need and the people we love.

My Ghazal Journey

Ghazals are unnatural for me, perhaps because I can't help but look for linear connections. I'm also a rule follower. The interesting thing about this form is that while there are very precise rules, they lend themselves to a lot of freedom. Ghazals put me in a strange limbo, which is probably a good thing. All writers should spend some time wandering the tracks between stations. It's a confusing place to be, and it can feel dangerous, but it's what strengthens our skills.

Ghazals are about longing for what ultimately cannot be attained, and I think about that when I see people absorbed in their screens. I should know—I'm among the worst. Hanging out on social media can be a great way to connect and unwind. But it can also suck me in like a vortex as I scroll for hours while avoiding other tasks. What, exactly, are we hoping to find with such fervent, sustained attention?

I started a ghazal by placing the blame on a teenager. With three teens in my house, it was tempting to do.

Phone Ghazal

A girl on a sofa caresses a phone.
OMG, she Snaps, *she got dressed by her phone?*

So many stories to funnel through fingers,
so much life to press into a phone.

Rain, snow, blooms spatter the windows.
A boy looks down, possessed by his phone.

Do our hearts wither in that cold silver blood,
shrink in the pulsating excess of phone?

A damselfly alights on a screen in the garden.
Shoo it and tweet. Impress the phone.

Something good can come, like always.
Have you not found light's recess in your phone?

A holy man lingers at a T. Mobile stand.
They open accounts, and he blesses the phones.

A woman says she will die tonight,
unless she finds peace, unless hope in the phone.

The poet avoids the waiting room walls.
I can't look up, she'll confess to her phone.

Writing this ghazal, and others that followed, piqued my mind
to play with possibilities: nine different images prompted by
the internal rhyme and ending word of *phone.* When I consider
the fact that I'm looking at a phone through nine different
train station windows, it's no wonder the process drives me to
explore the subject at deeper levels. Since I can't rely on narrative but must return to the lyrical structure and sound in
each couplet, I find myself embodying eight different worlds
until ending with my own—*the poet* and her own hapless habit.

Your Leg of the Trip

First, a quick recap of how to craft the ghazal form:

- Every line is traditionally the same length and follows a consistent metrical pattern
- Minimum of five stanzas
- Each stanza includes two lines, making a couplet
- Each couplet should be able to stand alone, as if it were its own poem
- In the first couplet, known as the *matla,* both lines end with the same word/refrain (*radif*)
- The matla also introduces a rhyme (*qafia*) **inside** the line, right before the radif (which always ends the line where it appears)
- The qafia and radif will now repeat on every **second** line of every remaining couplet
- The last couplet will include the poet's name or other reference to the self. This self-reference is sometimes humorous or odd

Ready? All aboard!

1. Write a line that engages you, stirs you. That might feel a bit like you're grabbing something out of the air, but remember, the ghazal is about longing for the beloved, whoever or whatever that might be. To get you thinking, journal your response to any or all of the prompts below:

    -An unfulfilled dream

    -A person you've lost touch with

-An idea you had or emotion you felt while reading a
book

-Something you wish you could go back and redo

-Something you want to understand better about
another person

-Something you want to believe but just can't

Write about one of these longings for a while—maybe
10 or 15 minutes. Then find an image that grabs you
and turn it into a poetic line.

2. Write and rewrite the line until the language rings for
you. When choosing the wording, keep the rhyme
(qafia) and refrain (radif) in mind. This is where real
craft comes in. You don't want the rhyme to control
everything, but you want it to work.

Here's an example. Let's say I journaled about something I wish I could go back and redo—in this case,
never allowing my kids within ten feet of a smartphone.
Okay, maybe that's not realistic. But longings usually
aren't. Here's a portion of my journaling:

> *She used to spend the whole day reading and dressing up,
> but now she's on her phone all day, lying on the couch as
> if there's nothing else in the world. I wish I could go back
> and tell her she'd have her whole life to do this. I wish I'd
> put my foot down a little longer.*

I choose these words to craft into a line:

> *She's on her phone all day, lying on the couch.*

On their own, the words don't present a very engaging
rhyme or refrain. I want to end my line with a flexible
qafia (rhyme) and strong radif (refrain) worthy of repeating for at least four more stanzas. (In other words, this

may not be the best occasion to use —you guessed it—
orange.)

So let me do this:

She lies around with her phone all day.

Do I want to focus on day so much? Is that really the
object of my longing or source of my emotions?

Let me try this:

A girl lies on the couch with her phone.

Phone is a better word to keep coming back to, especially
since returning to the phone over and over is the literal
problem. But what internal rhyme will I use? *With?* Meh.
Couch? (Calculating possible rhymes in my head...*slouch?*
Grouch? Maybe.)

Or this:

A girl on a sofa caresses a phone.

Bingo.

3. Now here comes the fun part. List as many rhymes
   as you can, to possibly combine with the refrain.
   Going through a rhyming dictionary or app is extremely
   helpful. When I was younger, I thought rhyming dic-
   tionaries were a form of cheating. Whatever. Never.
   Here are all the options I came up with:

   Messes...phone

   Blesses...phone

   Dresses...phone

   Guesses...phone

   Presses...phone

   Accesses...phone

   Excesses...phone

   Recesses...phone

Obsesses…phone
Stresses…phone
Addresses…phone
Confesses…phone
Expresses…phone
Coalesces…phone
Depresses…phone
Impresses…phone
Possesses…phone
Regresses…phone
Successes…phone
Compresses…phone
Progresses…phone

The little connecting words, like articles and prepositions, can come later. This is my main list of rhymes, and I will use it to create phrases with *phone* for my couplets.

4. Use your bank of rhyme/refrain phrases to write your couplets. Your first line doesn't have to rhyme or repeat any words, but it has to work with your qafia and radif (rhyme and refrain) in the next line and be a similar length. This is where the fun possibilities come into play.

5. Refer to yourself, somehow, in the last couplet. Poets have used their name, nickname, or descriptive words to refer back to the self. Incidentally, there's something humbling and instructive about bringing the poem back to yourself at the end. Go with those feelings.

6. Celebrate. Run through the fields like a gazelle (the

beautiful animal whose name, incidentally, derives from—you guessed it—ghazal, Arabic for love poem). You did it. You wrote a ghazal.

Go the Extra Mile (Try Ghazal Meters)

In traditional ghazals, each line follows the same meter, so the poem can easily be put to music; the syllable pattern then corresponds to the beat of the music. Like Greek meter, which we'll cover in the "Go the Extra Mile" section on odes, Urdu meter (known as *beher*) focuses on long and short syllables, rather than stressed and unstressed ones. (You can hop forward to Odes, if you want a rundown of what "long and short syllables" are all about—with explanations, examples, and discussion of the possibilities for how to write meter meant for one language in a language that works according to different rules. Don't worry, I'll wait. If you just want to read on, it can help to know that a long syllable is one that takes about twice as long to say as a short syllable (think of the difference between "uh" and "uhhh"). Notation-wise, "u" is a short syllable, while "—" is a long syllable, and "/" just stands for the break between feet).

In most of these meters, which end on a long syllable, you can add a short syllable at the end of an individual line if it works better for the poem (just as, with iambic pentameter—ten syllables that always end on a stress—you can sometimes vary your lines with a "feminine ending" by adding an eleventh unstressed syllable).

The meters below are only a very few of the many different behers used to write a ghazal. The names have been simplified here to only the overarching form, without including their particular variant. If you're interested in going further in learning about Urdu poetry and meter, you can read *Urdu Meter: A Practical Handbook,* by Frances W. Pritchett and Khaliq Ahmad Khaliq, online at Columbia.edu.

Some Ghazal Meters

— — — / — u — / u — — (*hazaj*)

— — / u — — / / — — — / u — — (*mutaqaarib*)

— — u — / — — — u — / — — — u — / — — — u — (*rajaz*)

— u — — / — u — — / — u — — / — u — (*ramal*)

— u — / — u — / — u — / — (*mutadaarik*)

u — — — / u — — — / u — — — / u — — —

> (Another hazaj. This version can't have an extra short syllable at the end.)

To write a ghazal, choose one of the meters, and compose each line of the ghazal so it follows the same pattern throughout the poem. You can either "translate" the meters to an English stressed/unstressed definition, or try to keep the long/short syllable focus (for more ideas on that count, check out Odes). You may find that it is quite difficult to move this effort from Urdu to English, due to the different ways the languages work. That's okay. The fun is in the playful trying.

6

Pantoums Come in With the Tide

A pantoum is an incantation. More interwoven than a villanelle, but adhering to a tighter "story," say, than a ghazal, it creates an interlocking chain of sound and ideas that shift with each encounter.

Mark Strand and Eavan Boland describe the form as one in which "the reader takes four steps forward, then two back...a perfect form for the evocation of a past time." Edward Hirsch personifies the pantoum as "always looking back over its shoulder," again, concerning itself with past times, loss, or regret. On the other hand, incanting the past can also bring about opportunities for reflection and hope. With their constant turning back on themselves, pantoums cover a range of emotions.

The pantoum originated in Malaysia as an oral poem known as a *pantun* that became popular throughout the world. These poems are flexible—they can be both a fancy, high-art form, and an everyday folk poem, and anywhere from a couplet (two lines), to a group of four quatrains (four-line stanzas) that's sixteen total lines in length. The pantun tends to have an ABAB rhyme scheme.

One particular variant on the pantun, where certain lines repeat across stanzas, following a pattern, is known as *pantun berkait*—or, in English, as a pantoum.

The standard pantoum consists of quatrains, where the

second and fourth lines of each stanza repeat as the first and third lines in the stanza that follows, like the entire poem is scrolling down as you read.

Stanza one lines:
1
2
3
4
Stanza two lines:
2
5
4
6
Stanza three lines:
5
7
6
8

This pattern continues for any number of stanzas, switching it up in the final stanza, in which the last line grabs the first line from the first stanza and the second line grabs the third line from the first stanza. (Basically, it switches up the simple "scroll down" formula by changing the direction those first two lines appear in—line three appears *first*, and line one appears at the *end,* so the poem ends on the same line it started with.)

Here, then, are the final-stanza lines for our four-stanza example (remember, pantoums can be any number of stanzas!):

Stanza four lines:

7

3

8

1

In Natasha Trethewey's pantoum "Incident," the form lends to the haunting quality of a terrifying memory that returns.

Incident

We tell the story every year—
how we peered from the windows, shades drawn—
though nothing really happened,
the charred grass now green again.

We peered from the windows, shades drawn,
at the cross trussed like a Christmas tree,
the charred grass still green. Then
we darkened our rooms, lit the hurricane lamps.

At the cross trussed like a Christmas tree,
a few men gathered, white as angels in their gowns.
We darkened our rooms and lit hurricane lamps,
the wicks trembling in their fonts of oil.

It seemed the angels had gathered, white men in their gowns.
When they were done, they left quietly. No one came.
The wicks trembled all night in their fonts of oil;
by morning the flames had all dimmed.

When they were done, the men left quietly. No one came.
Nothing really happened.
By morning all the flames had dimmed.
We tell the story every year.

—Natasha Trethewey

Handling the pantoum differently than Trethewey does, David K. Wheeler chooses to incorporate rhyme. While rhyme is not a requirement by modern definitions, poets still sometimes employ it to enhance the lilting effect of repetition—in this case, a somber lullaby.

Lullaby for the Sunshine Silver Mine

Fire Sweeps Idaho Silver Mine;
Several Dead and Many Missing
New York Times *headline, May 3, 1972*

Close your heavy eyes a while,
just hear the caged canary sing
as the mountain pyre ambles by.
Fix your muffled ears on listening.

Just hear the caged canary sing
for all the widows weeping at home.
Fix your muffled ears on listening
for your breath sweeping against the stone.

For all the widows weeping at home

know now that the workers won't return;
for your breath sweeping against the stone
is all that keeps your head alert.

Know now that the workers won't return.
The canary's song, wilting,
is all that keeps your head alert,
your heart awake, and your fingers warm.

The canary's song, wilting,
echoes deep in the smothered, gravel shaft.
Your heart, awake, and your fingers, warm,
are soon undone by the anoxic drafts.

Echoes deep in the smothered, gravel shaft
calm the canaries, and mind. The Bitterroots
are soon undone by the anoxic drafts.
Unloose the strings from your bulky boots.

Calm the canaries, and mind the Bitterroots
as the mountain pyre ambles by.
Unloose the strings from your bulky boots.
Close your heavy eyes a while.

—David K. Wheeler

This pantoum by Chip Livingston uses the form to mirror the movement of ocean tides and its creatures, a subject we will talk about soon.

Punta del Este Pantoum

Accept my need and let me call you brother,
Slate blue oyster, wet sand crustacean,
In your hurrying to burrow, wait. Hover.
Parse opening's disaster to creation's

Slate, to another blue-eyed monstrous sand crustacean,
Water-bearer. Hear the ocean behind me,
Pursued, asking to be opened, asking Creation
To heed the tides that uncover you nightly.

Water-bearer, wear the water beside me,
Hide your burying shadow from the shorebirds,
But heed the tides that uncover you nightly.
Gems in sandcastles, stick-written words,

Hidden from the shadows of shorebirds,
Washed over by water. Waters revelatory
Gems, sand, castles, sticks, words—
Assured of erasure, voluntary erosion.

Watched over with warrior resolution,
Crab armor, claws, and nautilus heart,
Assured of a savior, reconstruct your evolution,
Clamor to hear, water scarab, what the tampered heart hears.

A scarab's armor is light enough to fly.
In your hurry to burrow, wait. Hover.

Hear the clamor of the crustacean's heart.
Heed this call of creation. Call me brother.

—Chip Livingston

Catch a Pantoum

People are mesmerized by ocean waves. They love to walk by them, play in them, lie on blankets near them, ride them, and pay top dollar to live near them. Waves come in a number of forms, including surface waves, wind waves, and dreaded tsunamis, and even those can be divided into a multitude of classifications. But for the sake of writing poetry, let's imagine for a moment the gentle, consistent waves of the ocean lapping the shore on a calm day at the beach.

As a kid growing up in California near the beach, I wasn't a big swimmer. In fact, I didn't really learn to successfully cross a pool till around the age of 12. So I spent a lot of time standing in the sand letting the waves wash over my toes. And I was okay with that.

Waves blend into each other. That's one reason people love to watch and listen to them. They form a soothing rhythm that has been compared to the sounds within the womb.

But they also differ enough to surprise and delight.

Even when waves look mostly the same, they come in bringing treasures that can never be duplicated: a shell, a hunk of kelp, a tiny crab, a spark of sea glass. If we pay really close attention, we can even find different shapes in the foam.

Pantoums are like that. A line washes over us, goes back out to sea, and comes back, but perhaps bearing a surprise, like those tiny, pointed spiral shells no bigger than a joint on my pinkie finger. Even a different glint of light.

Pantoums are also often compared to chains, and it's no surprise why. Lines act as links between stanzas, and even the last stanza links back to the first by repeating lines 1 and 3. But unlike most chains, the pantoum is more colorful and, shall we say—fluid?—like waves.

My Pantoum Journey

I have found that writing a pantoum really does activate my looking-over-the-shoulder posture. Perhaps the best illustration of engaging with a pantoum is standing in the waves and gazing back, hair blowing in the wind (just to make it a little more Instagram worthy).

While the pantoum is cited as one of the best forms for dealing with the past, you don't have to approach it with the past all figured out. In fact, in my pantouming process, I have found that starting with a few stirring lines is enough to take me back to where the poem needs to go. It's quite freeing, for the lines create the past I didn't know I needed to find.

In the following pantoum, I started with this pretty straightforward memory from my childhood:

> I stabbed the Victorian coffee table
> with the blunt lead of a pencil
> for no reason other than wonder.
> Could something so sumptuous break. . .

I'm not sure why this image came to mind during one of my

writing sessions. I haven't seen that table in years, or if I have during one of my visits to my mom's house, I don't remember. But for some reason, the memory presented itself, so I allowed the waves to do their work.

> with the blunt lead of a pencil,
> bear a sudden, fierce hacking from 1982?
> Something sumptuous broke
> to make it: a red mahogany tree
>
> bore the sudden, fierce hacksaw of 1882.
> Forest to carriage, studio, and parlor.
> They made a red mahogany tree
> carry its memory of leaves...

Quite naturally, the form brought me back to a century before the ill-fated stabbing and prompted me to imagine the table before it was a table by varying the line ending *1982* with the year 1882. Slight variations are okay in pantoums. Think about those ocean waves coming in with different shades of light.

By picking up these lines again, I go out and come back in with the tide:

> from its forest to the carriage, studio, and parlor
> where the lustrous curved edges
> carried the carved memory of leaves
> beneath shimmering martinis.

Those lustrous curved edges
lived for a hundred years
beneath shimmering martinis
and just like that, I poked holes

in a hundred years trying to live
out their slow, seasoned decadence.
Just like that, I filled the holes
with smushed brown chapstick. No one noticed.

The slow seasons and decades
of guilt never brought me to confess
the smushed brown chapstick, and no one noticed.
Some things are better left unknown.

The poet Seth Haines writes that "poetic forms can bring an explorative freedom to the poet. But if we view them as burdens or cumbersome forms, we may avoid them and miss an opportunity to learn something new about ourselves or the stories around us." Notice a theme yet? Form brings a freedom you didn't know you lacked. By being "compelled" to repeat lines, you find yourself exploring different emotions more deeply than you might have in a free verse poem. You may find yourself turning those spiral shells a bit more slowly in your hand.

I ended up titling the above poem "Pantoum of Confession" because that is indeed what it became, sort of. Let's just say I won't be giving my mom a copy of this book.

Your Leg of the Trip

First, a quick recap of how to craft the pantoum form:

- Use quatrains, as many as you like
- Repeat the second and fourth lines of each stanza as the first and third lines in the stanza that follows

  Stanza one lines: **1 2** *3* **4**
  Stanza two lines: **2** 5 **4** 6
  Stanza three lines: 5 7 6 8

- In the final stanza, the first and third lines from the opening stanza are finally re-used, but in the opposite order. Line 3 appears *before* line 1—so the poem ends with the same line with which it started

  Final stanza lines: [#] *3* [#] **1**

Pantoums are often grouped with villanelles because both forms work with repeating lines. Our villanelle exercise, however, asked for a little more upfront work of choosing lines, brainstorming rhyming words, and tweaking as necessary before fully committing to refrains. The pantoum is a bit of a discover-as-you-go process. When you start off with that first stanza, all you know is that lines 1 and 3 will end up in the final stanza at some point. That's okay. Imagine yourself standing on the beach. Let go.

1. Catch a memory, any memory. It can be a big event or something as seemingly small as poking a table with a

pencil. Just make sure you give yourself sensory detail to work with. Pantoums based in abstraction often tend to blow across the surface of the mind like seafoam.

2. Write your first four-line stanza. Remember, you don't need to worry about rhyme in a contemporary pantoum. However, keep good line breaks in mind. It is always better to end on a clear verb, noun, or adjective than an article or preposition, especially when the line is going to show up again.

3. Grab the third and first lines of that stanza and deposit them as placeholders at the bottom of the page, where they will become the second and fourth lines of the last stanza.

4. Dive into the waves of your pantoum, repeating lines two and four of each successive stanza as one and three in the stanzas that succeed them, for however many stanzas you want to go. Unlike the villanelle, sonnet, or sestina, there is no limit to the number of stanzas.

5. To vary your options, and to add interest to your pantoum, play with the forms or meanings of words or punctuation as you repeat lines. For example, in the last two stanzas of my "Pantoum of Confession," I vary *out their slow, seasoned decadence* with *the slow seasons and decades. Decadence* and *decades* don't even share the same word root, but they echo one another in sound.

> in a hundred years trying to live
> **out their slow, seasoned decadence.**
> Just like that, I filled the holes
> with smushed brown chapstick. No one noticed.

The slow seasons and decades
of guilt never brought me to confess
the smushed brown chapstick, and no one noticed.
Some things are better left unknown.

Pantoumists also vary lines by switching syntax around in repeated phrases. In fact, I'm not sure if you can survive a pantoum without doing so! Take a look at Wheeler's line *for all the widows weeping at home,* which first appears as a prepositional phrase at the end of a sentence but reappears in the next stanza as an introductory clause.

Just hear the caged canary sing
for all the widows weeping at home.
Fix your muffled ears on listening
for your breath sweeping against the stone.

For all the widows weeping at home
know now that the workers won't return;
for your breath sweeping against the stone
is all that keeps your head alert.

6. As always, read your poem aloud several times to see what you could tweak to improve the flow.

Go the Extra Mile (Try a Pantun)

Travel back in pantoum time, and try your hand at the original form: *pantun.*

Like other short forms of poetry, such as haiku, the pantun works through embedding any number of allusions, shorthand references, and image-based language into its few lines. This image-based allusion and shorthand is key. Through it, the pantun draws connections between an event-image and a life concept.

Many pantun are about good deeds, love, nature, or moral advice, and they are often similar to proverbs and jokes. Altogether, these traditional verses have created a canon used in references, other writing, and in everyday conversation.

Most pantun are a single quatrain with an ABAB rhyme scheme, though they can also have an AAAA rhyme scheme, or even an AA rhyme scheme, for the shorter, couplet version. Full rhymes aren't required; half rhymes are totally okay!

Split your four (or two) lines of the pantun into two segments. The first half of the poem, the *pembayang* (foreshadower), will start the poem with a symbolic scene or event from nature, to set up the poem. The second half of the poem, the *maksud* (meaning), will answer the first half more concretely, bringing your poem toward the situation it's meant to convey.

"To enjoy the pantun one must learn something of its special symbols, just as one has to learn the meaning of many gestures to understand the language of mime in classical ballet," says Katherine Sim, as Cliff Goddard quotes in his study of active metaphors. You could try researching to learn about these special pantun symbols, then bring them into your own pantun.

Here is a sample:

A cane of sugar on a far-off shore
brims with amber from root to crown.

How crystal sweet are the words that pour
their lush deceptions to take you down.

—Anonymous, translated by L.L. Barkat

To explore the pantun form, start with your ABAB quatrain, and choose a general idea you want to convey. Write in a fixed rhythm of between eight to twelve syllables for each line. To keep true to the spirit of this short, reference-rich poem, try to convey your ideas through:

- well-known imagery
- allusion to historical events
- allusion to well-known people
- references to popular stories that are easy to "get the point" of (urban myths, fairy tales, superhero comics, etc.)
- well-known sayings
- places
- words that call to mind other words
- established symbols

7

The Rondeau Gets Around

On second thought, maybe not. The rondeau doesn't often make it to the top of the list of forms—or even to the top five or ten—and that's too bad. Because it's awesome. Challenging, perhaps, but awesome. In fact, what I love most about the form is how effortlessly it flows for the reader, without letting on that the poet has done quite a bit of legwork to pull it off. This is not to worry you. I have full confidence you can write one of these gems, or several.

Now for its anatomy: The rondeau started as a song form with the French troubadours in the 12th and 13th centuries, eventually becoming popularized as a literary form by poet and composer Guillame de Machaut in the 14th century. Used in modern-day English, the rondeau is a poem of 15 lines of eight or ten syllables arranged in three stanzas—the first stanza is five lines (*quintet*), the second is four lines (*quatrain*), and the final stanza is six lines (*sestet*).

The first half of the first line becomes the rondeau's *rentrement,* or refrain, when it is repeated as the last line of each of the two succeeding stanzas. Only two other rhymes are used in the whole poem. The entire scheme looks like this (with "R" used to indicate the rentrement):

AABBA AABR AABBAR

Get it? Maybe not. Like so many forms, it's challenging to really comprehend it without seeing it and, even more, *hearing it,* for yourself. The most well-known rondeau, hands down, is "In Flanders Fields," written by the Canadian soldier John McCrae on the battlefront in Ypres, Belgium, during WWI:

In Flanders Fields

In Flanders fields the poppies blow
Between the crosses, row on row,
    That mark our place; and in the sky
    The larks, still bravely singing, fly
Scarce heard amid the guns below.

We are the Dead. Short days ago
We lived, felt dawn, saw sunset glow,
    Loved and were loved, and now we lie
      In Flanders fields.

Take up our quarrel with the foe:
To you from failing hands we throw
    The torch; be yours to hold it high.
    If ye break faith with us who die
We shall not sleep, though poppies grow
      In Flanders fields.

—John McCrae

Read it aloud several times. It's easy to pick up on the form's foundation in song, because even without a melody, the rondeau sings.

The most challenging aspect of writing *rondeaux* (that's the plural form of rondeau) is finding an opening line worth repeating—and repeating just half of it, at that—and selecting two rhyme sounds that offer enough word choices. We'll talk about some strategies that can help, later in the chapter.

Here's a more contemporary rondeau by Rick Maxson, which, quite appropriately, happens to focus on song. Again, read it aloud and feel the rondeau work its musical magic:

Please Stay

I heard you singing in the next room,
sporadic—a disordered tune,
and behind the notes, the water ran,
the grace of clinking plates, your hands
warm water soothed, and thus the tune.

Through open windows a sort of choir
attended you and it seemed conspired
to fill each space, like time with sand.
I heard you singing

and knew that pain might stop you soon,
slant your peace toward gloom,
but for now please stay in whatever land
your song exists, like some magic wand
transported you, where in some soothing room
I heard you singing.

—Rick Maxson

Let's Circle Back

Road trips aren't all carnival rides and lighthouses. No matter how delightful the journey, there will undoubtedly be some bothersome realities along the way, like having to get bathroom keys from gas station attendants and forgetting to take your sunglasses off in a tunnel. Another reality of driving is encountering the rather controversial road feature known as a roundabout.

I know. I'm trying to *increase* the rondeau's popularity, so perhaps talking about roundabouts isn't the best strategy. However, I can't help myself. *Rondeau,* after all, is named after the French word for *round,* and what's rounder than a roundabout?

If you've never been on a roundabout, it's a bit of a mini-traffic circle that forces cars to travel slowly in a circle, in one direction, until reaching their chosen exits. Cars within the circle have the right of way, and others enter when they have an opening.

In busy areas, roundabouts improve traffic flow and prevent serious collisions by removing the dangers of high-speed intersections. The controversy comes from the fact that many motorists aren't used to them and get stressed out about how to enter and leave the circle.

That's the thing about the rondeau. It flows—or at least it's supposed to, once you get into it. Like a car that needs to pay attention to how to enter the circle, the rondeau can be smooth sailing until reaching the exit, which, incidentally, looks a lot like the entrance.

Entering a rondeau with a strong and repeatable opening

phrase is key to getting into the flow, as is setting up a good rhyme scheme that keeps you moving. (Never, I mean, never stop in the middle of a roundabout!) If you go around the circle more than once, as many out-of-towners do as they look for their exit, you'll keep coming back to the beginning. It's that repeated phrase that makes the rondeau a true circle. McCrae's poem is clearly defined by those Flanders fields.

My Rondeau Journey

Let me tell you about my first experience with rondeaux.

Really, let me tell you.

About a million years ago, when I started my MFA program in creative writing, I took a form class, and my very first assignment—there were still summer flowers in bloom—was to write a rondeau. I had never written one and was immediately drawn to the song-like quality of the form.

I no longer have the full text of the poem, but it was a lullaby of sorts, in which the planets speak to a child. *Let us tell you of the home we know* was the first line, with the refrain *let us tell you* repeated twice.

My professor hated it. She thought the poem was corny and cartoonish and said so in front of my fellow students. I was mortified and pledged from that moment forward to become more "gritty" in my writing. I spent the rest of the semester digging into the deep, dark secrets of my adolescence rather than animating Saturn's rings. But a classmate of mine never forgot the poem's refrain, and even today, more than a quarter century later, quotes it to me. My rondeau must have done something right, let me tell you.

Speaking of a quarter century, my husband and I recently celebrated our twenty-fifth anniversary, and I thought a rondeau would be the perfect poetic way to capture the quickness and timelessness of being together so long. At only 15 lines, a rondeau goes by quickly, but its rhyme scheme and refrain can get in your head and last forever. And in a shout-out to my first rondeau, I bring back some space imagery. Take that, professor!

Anniversary Rondeau

Twenty-five years is not so long
in the larger scheme of stars gone
to the cosmic recycling bin
or the bristlecone whistling wind
through its millennia-old prongs.

But we have outlasted a throng
of expired batteries, two strong
doses of tetanus each, in
twenty-five years:

a silver sliver that belongs
on the sugar tip of the tongue,
even when we search our chins
for epochal wrinkles, chagrined
and in love with the fast, slow song,
twenty-five years.

Your Leg of the Trip

First, a quick recap of how to craft the rondeau form:

- 15 lines—three stanzas of eight or ten syllables. The first stanza is a *quintet* (five lines), the second a *quatrain* (four lines), and the final stanza a *sestet* (six lines)
- The first half of the first line becomes the rondeau's *rentrement* (refrain), repeated on its own as the last line of each of the two succeeding stanzas
- Rhyme scheme: AABBA AABR AABBAR, with R standing for the refrain

Okay, so how do you make such a highly-prescribed form work? Here are some ways to get started.

1. Choose a subject that embodies a timeless quality for you. Unlike, say, a haiku (we'll get to those in a couple chapters), a rondeau is more than an impression or snapshot. While, yes, the rondeau's intensely lyrical form lends itself to big ideas like romance or mourning, don't rely on a purely abstract topic. For example, planning to write a rondeau about "love" is going to set you up for vagueness. Rick Maxson's rondeau is about *big ideas* of love and loss, but the *subject* that represents those ideas is a flesh-and-blood loved-one singing at the kitchen sink.
2. Begin freewriting about your subject. Set a timer for anywhere between five and ten minutes, and just write whatever comes to mind with no stopping or editing.

3. Read through your writing and highlight or underline phrases that have a "ring" for you. In the process of freewriting, you may have discovered that you actually want to write about something else. That's okay!

4. Choose and/or modify a phrase that a) is eight syllables long and b) has a four-syllable opening phrase that's worth repeating twice—including at the end of your poem. This will probably be the toughest part of putting together your rondeau. Experiment, take your time, and be prepared for the fact that it may change during the composition process.

5. Start listing as many words as you can that rhyme with that opening line's end rhyme. You'll be calling upon those words later. This is a similar approach to what you did with the ghazal. Brainstorming rhymes beforehand is not cheating but smart planning that gives your imagination a place to go.

6. Start writing that first stanza, keeping your lines at eight syllables each while also staying conscious of line 3's end-rhyme. That will become end-rhyme B. The rhyme should be versatile enough, like rhyme A, to be repeated, but different enough from A to provide a nice sonic contrast.

7. List some words for your end-rhyme B bank.

8. Knock out the rest of the poem. Like the rondeau itself, and our beloved roundabout, the process can take you in circles. You may end up changing the refrain and even changing rhymes. The syllable count may make you use words you wouldn't have considered before. This is one beauty of writing in form.

9. To help you stay organized, consider using a template, such as the following, courtesy of E.V. Wyler from *The Society of Classical Poets:*

Line 1: End-rhyme "A" — four-syllable opening phrase
     + four syllables = eight syllables
Line 2: End-rhyme "A" — eight syllables
Line 3: End-rhyme "B" —   "   "
Line 4: End-rhyme "B" —   "   "
Line 5: End-rhyme "A" —   "   "
Line 6: End-rhyme "A" — eight syllables
Line 7: End-rhyme "A" —   "   "
Line 8: End-rhyme "B" —   "   "
Line 9: Refrain (line 1's four-syllable opening phrase)
Line 10: End-rhyme "A" — eight syllables
Line 11: End-rhyme "A" —   "   "
Line 12: End-rhyme "B" —   "   "
Line 13: End-rhyme "B" —   "   "
Line 14: End-rhyme "A" —   "   "
Line 15: Refrain (line 1's four-syllable opening phrase)

10. Read your rondeau aloud, over and over, until it sings.

Go the Extra Mile (Try a Triolet, Rondel, and Rondelet)

The rondeau has gone round and round so much that it has a plethora of variant forms. Try your hand at any of the following…

Triolet: This older variant on the rondeau tends to have eight lines, and its rhyme scheme is ABaAabAB (capitals are the refrains—the repeated lines). The English version is usually written in iambic tetrameter. What's iambic tetrameter? It's a line made up of four (that's the *tetra* part) iambic feet. So: da-DUM da-DUM da-DUM da-DUM. Here is a sample triolet:

> When first we met we did not guess
> That Love would prove so hard a master;
> Of more than common friendliness
> When first we met we did not guess
> Who could foretell this sore distress,
> This irretrievable disaster
> When first we met? We did not guess
> That Love would prove so hard a master.

—Robert Bridges

Rondel: Usually a poem with eight-syllable lines, of either 13 or 14 lines. Unlike the rondeau, it has two refrains, which are a full line every time they appear (even the first time). Take a look at the rhyme scheme: ABba abAB abbaA(B). (Capital letters here stand for a refrain.) That final B, in parentheses? Means that you can do with or without the line, depending on your mood! The example below was originally written in French and now in English has several slant rhymes, wherever a full rhyme could not be adequately found to reproduce the original sound and meaning. (They are: *maid* and *riverside; way* and *maid; flutes* and *white; tied* and *light*).

Lady Moon Launders

Like a ghostly washing maid
softly splashing stains white,
bare arms silver-bright
singing along the riverside—

the meadow's winds make their way,
blow in their reedless flutes
like a ghostly washing maid
softly splashing stains white.

Heaven's so-sweet maid,
skirt upon her hips tied
under the branches, kissed light
her moon linens now outlaid
like a ghostly washing maid.

—Albert Giraud, translation by L.L. Barkat

Rondelet: A "small circle," this is a mini version. The rhyme scheme is AbAabbA, with A being the four-syllable refrain. All the other lines are the usual eight syllables—unless the poet chooses otherwise, as in the poem below. (Do you see the refrain trick Luders plays by including the title in the rondelet?)

A Rondelet

Is just seven verses rhymed on two.
A rondelet

Is an old jewel quaintly set
In poesy—a drop of dew
Caught in a roseleaf. Lo! For you,
A rondelet.

—Charles Henry Luders

8

The Ode is a "Monumental" Task

First, let's get this out of the way. These days, an ode behaves more like a mode than a form, defined primarily by intent and tone rather than a prescribed rhyme scheme or meter. Forgive me for including odes in any case.

Odes are hard to miss. For one thing, they almost always include "Ode" or "To [Something]" in the title. Also, they are straightforward in their purpose of celebrating the qualities of a person, place, thing, or event.

All of this is not to say an ode can't be written in form. Pindar, the ancient Greek poet who made odes famous, employs a particular triadic structure for most of them, and the English Romantic odes range from Pindaric to Horatian to irregular in form. Here's a well-loved Keats poem, written in the uniform stanzas of the Horatian ode:

To Autumn

Season of mists and mellow fruitfulness,
  Close bosom-friend of the maturing sun;
Conspiring with him how to load and bless
  With fruit the vines that round the thatch-eves run;
To bend with apples the moss'd cottage-trees,
  And fill all fruit with ripeness to the core;
  To swell the gourd, and plump the hazel shells

With a sweet kernel; to set budding more,
And still more, later flowers for the bees,
Until they think warm days will never cease,
　For summer has o'er-brimm'd their clammy cells.

Who hath not seen thee oft amid thy store?
　Sometimes whoever seeks abroad may find
Thee sitting careless on a granary floor,
　Thy hair soft-lifted by the winnowing wind;
Or on a half-reap'd furrow sound asleep,
　Drowsed with the fume of poppies, while thy hook
　Spares the next swath and all its twined flowers:
And sometimes like a gleaner thou dost keep
　Steady thy laden head across a brook;
　Or by a cider-press, with patient look,
　Thou watchest the last oozings, hours by hours.

Where are the songs of Spring? Ay, where are they?
　Think not of them, thou hast thy music too,—
While barred clouds bloom the soft-dying day,
　And touch the stubble-plains with rosy hue;
Then in a wailful choir the small gnats mourn
　Among the river sallows, borne aloft
　Or sinking as the light wind lives or dies;
And full-grown lambs loud bleat from hilly bourn;
　Hedge-crickets sing; and now with treble soft
　The redbreast whistles from a garden-croft,
　And gathering swallows twitter in the skies.

—John Keats

Odes have persisted for centuries. Pablo Neruda, who won the Nobel Prize for Literature in 1971, wrote odes on everything from socks to tomatoes to sadness—and Sharon Olds, in her newest collection (called, um, *Odes*) praises the likes of wind, hip replacements, trilobites, and the San Francisco Bay. Yes, the possibilities are truly endless.

Here are three types of odes you can explore...

Pindaric

Named for the Greek poet Pindar in the 5th century BC, Pindaric odes were *triadic* (that is, they had three parts). They were performed by a chorus and dancers, with the *strophe* sung or chanted first, by a chorus moving east to west across a stage. The ode turned on the *antistrophe*, which was sung second, west to east. It concluded with the *epode*.

While you don't need to worry about memorizing dance moves, you do need to make sure that your strophe and antistrophe mirror one another with the same rhyme scheme, meter, and length. The epode, as the grand finale, gets to do its own thing, but it still has to rhyme. For example, in each of three sections of his "The Progress of Posey: A Pindaric Ode," Thomas Gray follows this pattern:

Stanza one (strophe): ABBACCDDEEFF
Stanza two (antistrophe): ABBACCDDEEFF
Stanza three (epode): AABBACCDEDEFGFGHH

Horatian

Named for the Roman poet Horace in the 1st century BC,

Horatian odes were formed by a series of stanzas with a consistent repeating structure: rhyme, meter, and length. Almost all of Horace's poems were broken into stanzas of four lines each. Unlike Pindar, Horace wrote in this lyric form on any number of subjects, and even strayed away from what we now think of as the essence of an ode: the lofty praise of its subject. Yes, he certainly wrote in that manner at times, but many of Horace's poems were more personal. As for theme and tone, his odes could take a turn away from the lofty and dip into the tragic, ironic, or petty. There were poems that complained about the poet's situation; there were poems that told mythical stories; and there were even poems that warned his friends not to make bad decisions.

When writing a variation on something established in another language, there is always a degree to which you can't reproduce the form. And that's even without taking into account the issue of its original context. Think of the Pindaric ode, originally written for a full chorus of singers and dancers. Would such a poem even *be* a poem, or more properly a song?

One of Horace's odes was also made to be sung, for a big event, but that may have been an exception, since there's no evidence that he put any of his other odes to music. With the Horatian ode, the key was that he wrote in metrical forms that make much more sense in ancient Greek, so his odes had a lyric consistency no matter what the subject or how he chose to tell it.

If you want to try an English "Horatian ode" you can take inspiration from Keats's "To Autumn" and his rhyme scheme ABAB CDEDCCE, for each stanza of the triad.

Irregular

These made their first appearance around the 17th century. Each stanza has its own particular structure and rhyme scheme, or perhaps none at all.

Ode to a Lost Sweater

I see it now
like a simple word
spoken into the wind.
Bright button
in our mother's palm
from a hand-me-down
we had each outgrown.
Wool deep red as embers
that smolder in a circle of stone,
and the scent of Grandma's roses,
her gracefully wrought cable stitch
moths in an attic barrel
had chewed until split.
I see it
like a phantom wound
knits itself a scar,
and a heart-spun word
chanted into the wind
calls down a star.

—Janet Aalfs

The following poem, quite different from "Ode to a Lost Sweater" in its subject and tone, shows just how versatile and wide-ranging the ode can be. Like most contemporary odes, it falls into the "irregular" category. However, even irregular odes are often several stanzas in length, or at least very detailed. They are not impressionistic, like haiku, but thoroughly descriptive of their subjects—even, shall we say, "over the top"?

Ode to Butter

Oh Slippery Sweet Remnant of Animal
Fat, who spun and spun to thick liquid magic,
I could take you on my tongue anytime, anywhere,
could drag you slowly along the corners
of Portuguese rolls, or sizzle a spat of you
in skillets of broccoli spears, asparagus,
filet mignon, or lightly breaded chicken.

Oh Luminous Yellow-White Orb, you pool
in the caverns of mashed potatoes, roll
in your sexy heat down the sides
of pancake stacks. My mother always said
I'd marry the first man who could watch
me eat sweet Jersey corn-on-the-cob without dying
of jealousy (or was it shame?) when you slide
down my chin like an unruly trail of holy oil,
collecting on my lips, my neck, my cleavage,
so warm, so bright, so much salt and husk.

At our church's chicken suppers, you flaunted
your Sunday best in tiny molded florets.

I would've popped you one by one into my mouth
if the pastor wasn't looking, would have taken you
whole on my tongue, rolled you around like a caramel.
But the holy ladies were crooning Amazing Grace
to a soundtrack in three-part harmony, so smearing
your lonely floral goodness on my dinner roll
was as lugubrious as I could get in the dimming light.

Oh Butter, Glorious One, Holiest of Condiments,
to me you are the whole meal, le crème de la crème,
my morning coffee, my evening dessert and everything
in between. Without you, I cannot walk the road
of French toast, steamed vegetables, or lemon pound cake.
In sticks, tubs, foil pads, squeezie bottles, or plastic squares,
I will love you until my dying breath, until my arteries clog
beyond repair. Yes Butter, my love, I would even die for you.

—Rebecca Lauren

Odeside Attraction

Odes remind me of the wild, colorful, and often downright
strange roadside monuments that pepper American highways.
From the World's Largest Thermometer in Baker, California;
to Cadillac Ranch in Amarillo, Texas; and the Hodag statue in
Rhinelander, Wisconsin (don't know what a Hodag is? Do an
Internet image search and prepare to be horrified), these attractions celebrate their creators' objects of affection with shameless glory.

When driving through Colorado on our way to an arts workshop in Santa Fe, New Mexico, my friends Jen and Dave and I were drawn in by a sign for the UFO Watchtower, a 10-foot-tall viewing platform, museum, and healing garden in the San Luis Valley of Colorado.

We paid $5 for the car and pulled into a dusty compound. I posed for a selfie with a Big Foot statue before entering the gift shop/museum building that provided quite a few interesting displays, including illustrations of "Entities Observed by Witnesses." (All these entities had the classic, large-browed alien heads.) Another sign claimed, as of our visit in August of 2019, that there had been 214 sightings from the tower since its opening in 2000. "In 2008," it read, "the majority of sightings were daytime—they were silver balls people were seeing everywhere." My friends and I signed the guest book, browsed the tzoches (I seriously regret not buying alien earrings), then headed out to the Vortex Garden.

This is where the ode to aliens really sings. According to the Watchtower, "There are two large Vortexes located on the east side of the Tower. A Vortex is described as an opening to a Parallel Universe which is full of energy. One of the Vortexes spins clockwise and the other spins counterclockwise." People are encouraged to leave tokens of energy among alien statues and metal saucers, and they are invited to receive energy as well. The range of objects left in the garden is breathtaking: pins, hats, antlers, Rubik's Cubes, My Little Pony® figurines, license plates, Frisbees®, and pens and toothbrushes stuck in the ground by the thousands.

You don't have to believe in aliens or a parallel universe to appreciate the audacious celebration going on here. A giant, defunct satellite dish painted with enormous alien eyes, the south-central Colorado mountains and clouds hovering behind it. Dave and Jen posing under a saucer between two four-foot aliens decked out in Mardi Gras beads, scarves, sunglasses, and American flags. Visitors gazing at the colors and textures bestrewing this hallowed ground, leaving objects of their own. There was so much to take in here—a new detail with every shift of the eyes.

This is what a good ode does. It rejoices over its subject and doesn't hold back. It transports you into its very essence until you become a part of it, finally trudging back to your car with your eyes skyward, looking for a silver ball in the sun.

My Ode Journey

Odes are the perfect outlet for writing shamelessly about our obsessions. While I may enjoy visiting the occasional alien monument and bonding there with my friends, I'm not what you would call a rabid fan. Music, however, is another story.

Having submerged myself in Celtic music over the past few years, I've decided to write a series of odes celebrating Irish musicians, many of whom dedicate themselves to instruments we don't find in most elementary school bands—such as bodhráns, bouzoukis, and uilleann pipes. I wanted to celebrate them by attempting to understand their language. While I am a musician, I have literally never touched a number of these instruments. Without enough time or money available to learn them, I've had to find fresh ways to encounter their essence.

Writing about music requires *ekphrasis,* or engaging a work of art through poetry. Without a visual form to hang onto, music writing almost always requires some sort of synesthesia, or mixing of senses, in order to tap into the spirit of a sound. Such an approach leads to figurative language, of course—a common feature of odes. When writing a poem of celebration, you must know how you're praising the subject and why, holding it to the light to inspect it from different angles. What results is a rich collection of colors and light—metaphor with, as Keats writes, "ripeness to the core."

So I not only listened to these instruments and watched their players both on video and in live performance, but interviewed some as well, including a couple of bodhrán players. Writing odes to musicians has helped me understand them and love their music even more.

Ode to a Bodhrán Player

Your left hand caresses the inner skin
    like the small of a lover's back.
Your right hand flicks the tipper—
        whomp-glug-clackclack-whomp—
jouncing with the dancers' ringlets
        as the goat stretched over the frame
scampers back to life
        among the fiddles and pipes.

I don't know my way without it,
        you say. And I understand
you mean more than the passage
        of a song. Your day winds through

the bodhrán beats like a current
　　　　　through stone. You hold on
when stormswept and pummeled
　　　　　and cold. Even when you sleep
you collect the silt that flickers off
　　　　　the jigs and reels,
heartbeat of light in your hair.

Your Leg of the Trip

First, a quick recap of how to craft the ode form:

- Odes are usually written to praise something in a lofty manner
- Pindaric odes, which tend to be about winning a sporting event, follow a triadic (three part) structure. The first two sections—the *strophe* and *antistrophe*—have the same rhyme scheme, length, and meter, while the *epode* (the final section) has a different rhyme scheme, length, and meter.

  A classic English adaptation of the Pindaric ode, created by Thomas Gray, uses the following rhyme scheme — strophe: ABBACDDEEFF; antistrophe: ABBACDDEEFF; epode: AABBACCDEDEFGFGHH
- Horatian odes can be about a wider variety of subjects, can be more personal, and don't even have to praise something. They also follow a triadic structure, but each stanza has the same rhyme scheme, length, and meter. They may have two- or four-line stanzas. Keats, adapting the idea of the Horatian ode, uses the rhyme scheme ABAB CDEDCCE for each stanza of "To Autumn"

- Irregular odes praise their subject matter but don't have a triadic structure or a standard rhyme scheme, length, or meter

Some of Pablo Neruda's best-loved poems are odes to every-day objects. Here are just a few of his prized subjects:

artichoke	dictionary	chowder
wood	lizard	soap
tomatoes	bicycles	spoon
socks	salt	scissors

While he also wrote odes to larger, more abstract subjects, such as sadness, solidarity, and the color green, he honored tangible objects in a way that has captured the imaginations of generations of readers and poets.

In Neruda-like fashion, brainstorm a list of the everyday objects in your life, but place them in three columns. In the first column, list those things you regularly acknowledge as subjects of your affection, such as coffee, hot showers, or your guitar. In the second column, list those common objects you don't normally think about so much, such as a rubber band or key. In the third column, list those everyday objects you dislike, such as mosquitos, floss, or junk mail.

Choose an object from each column and write an ode to each of them. (If time doesn't permit today, choose just one.) Looking back to the sample poems as examples, include plenty of sensory details and figurative language. Remember, imagery refers to more than just the sense of sight. Delve deeply into how your object sounds, feels, and, if applicable, smells and tastes. In order to keep with the traditionally elevated tone of an ode, address your subject directly. This will be a poem full of *You*, not *it*.

Why consider writing an ode to an object you feel neutral about, or even dislike? It's good for the imagination, of course. If you don't *actually* love that old weed whacker in the garage, pretending you do will make you a better poet. I can pretty much guarantee it.

Pindaric, Horatian, or irregular? The choice is yours.

Go the Extra Mile (Try Greek Meters)

Instead of stresses, Greek meter focused on long and short syllables, called *longum* and *brevis*. While this is not particularly intuitive for the English language, poems written in Greek meters (even if composed in English), have a markedly different sound and effect.

While the idea of a stressed or unstressed syllable is that a stressed syllable has more emphasis or weight than an unstressed syllable (like the iamb's da-DUM or the trochee's DUM-da), the idea of a long syllable is that it literally *takes longer to say* than a short syllable.

You'll soon see some examples of feet the Greeks would use to create metrical lines. Some of these have the same names you may have learned in the "stressed/unstressed" model. But, to read these feet and metrical structures, just remember that "—" stands for a longum (long) syllable, and "u" stands for a brevis (short) syllable.

For example, in the English stressed/unstressed model, both *inlet* and *smoothly* are trochees (stressed + unstressed).

But in Greek poetry (and Latin, for that matter) you aren't paying attention to stresses but length instead; under this model, converting to English, *inlet* would be a pyrrhic syllable (short + short), while *smoothly* is still a trochee—notice it takes **less time** to say the first part of *inlet (in)* than it does to say the first part of *smoothly (smooth).*

This isn't applicable to the normal use of English! Don't become confused by thinking English meter works this way. It doesn't. This model is only useful to know if you want to recapture the sound of Greek or Latin meter—as certain poets and play-wrights have tried.

There are two ways to go about converting a longum/bre-vis meter into English. One is to keep the pattern of the meter and replace long and short with the more familiar stressed and unstressed, as Tennyson did in his self-aware poem "Hen-decasyllabics:"

> Look, I come to the test, a tiny poem
> All composed in a metre of Catullus…

—u —uu— u— u— u

Another way is to try to replicate the meters with long and short syllables, rather than stressed and unstressed ones. For the sake of such poetic reading and writing we can draw from Latin rules to help transcribe a long syllable into English. A long syllable would be:

• A syllable with a long vowel (A as in *late;* E as in *meet;* I as in *might;* O as in *moat;* U as in *blue)*

- A dipthong (the bolded double vowels in l**ou**d, l**ie**d, l**ay**, l**oi**n, l**oo**n, l**ea**n, l**ee**r, l**ai**r)
- A short vowel plus more than one consonant (*a* as in *mast; e* as in *melt; i* as in *mist; o* as in *fond; u* as in *rust*)

You can try either method for your own poetry—or both! The most important part is to explore and have fun. There's no "wrong way" to do this kind of what-if experiment.

Here are some Greek feet to play around with. Try saying the following longum/brevis examples aloud, so you can hear the differences. (For the short part, just say a quick "uh" and for the long part, drag that out and say "uhhh.")

Disyllables
Pyrrhus: u u
Iamb: u —
Trochee: — u
Spondee: — —

Trisyllables
Tribrach: u u u
Dactyl: — u u
Amphibrach: u — u
Anapaest: u u —
Bacchius: u — —
Cretic: — u —
Antibacchius: — — u
Molossus: — — —

There are a bunch of longer feet, too, but I won't get into that except for these:

> Choriambus (or, choriamb): — u u —   [the choriamb is
>   literally: trochee (— u) + iamb (u —)]
> Choriambo-cretic (or dodrans): — u u — u — [a chori-
>   amb (—u u —) + iamb (u —)]

You can find a choriamb in English in these lines from Keats's
"To Autumn":

Who hath not **seen** thee oft amid thy store?

(**Who** is a long syllable, *hath not* are two short syllables, **seen**
is a long syllable.)

Greek meters take these feet and put them together in various patterns to create metrical schemes for different poems.
(This "//" stands for the *caesura,* or the part in the line where
you end one phrase and begin another, and "x" stands for a
place in the meter where you can put either a long or a short
syllable.)

Here are some Greek meters to play with:

Alcaic (Greek Version)

x — u — x — u u — u —

x — u — x — u u — u —

x — u — x — u — —

— u u — u u — u — —

Alcaic (Latin Version)

— — u — — // — u u — u —

— — u — — // — u u — u —

— — u — — — u — —

— u u — u u — u — —

Sapphic

— u — x — u u — u — —

— u — x — u u — u — —

— u — x — u u — u — —

— u u — —

You can also create a host of meters by combining different metrical lines together, like in the Asclepiadean meters. Each line below is a version of an Asclepiadean meter, which can be used in combination with the others to create poem forms. As you can see, these lines are primarily built around the choriamb (—u u —).

Asclepiadean metric lines

(G) Glyconic: x x — u u — u — (two free syllables + a choriamb + a trochee)

(A1) Lesser Asclepiad: x x — u u— — u u —u —
(two free syllables + a choriamb + a dodrans)

(A2) Greater Asclepiad: x x — u u — — u u — — u
u — u —

(P) Pherecratean: x x — u u — —

To write a poem in Asclepiadean meter the way Horace did, write in four-line stanzas, choosing an order and combination of these Asclepiadean lines to create your form. You don't have to use all these metric lines at once! You can use one, two, or three of the line forms, and repeat them in various patterns to get your four lines.

9

What Once Was Lost is Now a Found Poem

Looking for a poem? You can find it with *found poetry,* freedom at its finest. (Alliteration, anyone?) Found poetry is poetry you discover and recreate using texts written by someone else. It's fun, challenging (if you're doing it right), and full of surprises.

T. S. Eliot, famous for "finding" his own complex masterpieces such as "The Waste Land" in the depths of literary allusions and quotations, has this to say about borrowing text:

> Immature poets imitate; mature poets steal; bad poets deface what they take, and good poets make it into something better, or at least something different. The good poet welds his theft into a whole of feeling which is unique, utterly different from that from which it was torn; the bad poet throws it into something which has no cohesion.

But wait! Isn't all this stealing and welding *plagiarism?* Are these works publishable, since they contain other people's words? Are they still poems, since in most cases the text being lifted didn't start out as poetry? Is this fair use?

These are good questions. *The Found Poetry Review,* an online found-poetry journal that has sadly shuttered its doors but still keeps past issues and resources available, goes straight to the American University's Center for Social Media's "Code of

Best Uses in Fair Use for Poetry" for answers.

Here's a portion of what they say about writing "New Works 'Remixed' from Other Material: allusion, pastiche, centos, erasure, use of 'found' material, poetry-generating software":

> Under fair use, a poet may make use of quotations from existing poetry, literary prose, and non-literary material, if these quotations are re-presented in poetic forms that add value through significant imaginative or intellectual transformation, whether direct or (as in the case of poetry-generating software) indirect.

You may read the code in its entirety online, but, to summarize, found poetry is just fine as long as there is a clear attempt at "adding value through…transformation." In other words, **create.** Make something new. In the literal definition of the word, *re-present*. I have yet to meet an artist who wasn't honored by other people explicitly citing their work as inspiration for more art.

There are a number of types of found poetry, some of them mentioned by name in the code above.

Erasure

For this kind of found poetry, the poet takes an existing source and erases the majority of the text, leaving behind words that make a new poem. This is also known as "black out" poetry and can be done both physically and digitally. Austin Kleon has brought a lot of attention to this mode of found poetry with his book *Newspaper Blackout,* illustrating the imaginative power of redaction.

Here's an erasure poem Katie Manning wrote from the book of Ecclesiastes. I'm not kidding when I say erasurists take out a lot of text when making a new poem:

The Book of Class

all that remains of Ecclesiastes

the days
will say
find
pleasure in
the light
the clouds
the windows
the almond tree
the grasshopper
the streets
the sound of
people
afraid of heights

the dust returns to
meaning

find
the word
like firmly embedded nails
in
every hidden thing

—Katie Manning

The beautiful thing about erasure is that any poet using this ancient source text would come up with something new. The writing is in the finding.

Cut-up

In this rather therapeutic type of found poetry, the poet cuts or tears physical text into words and phrases then rearranges them to create a new poem. It's like erasure…but the opposite. The Dadaist Tristan Tzara started the practice by choosing words from a hat with which to write a poem. The technique was later popularized by Beat poet William Boroughs and even employed by David Bowie and Kurt Cobain when writing lyrics.

Here's a cut-up poem comprised of directives that poet Marci Rae Johnson found in women's magazines:

#DoDifferentDaily

Take the scenic route while developing
a contingency plan. Look

what's
inside… &

hang accessories
like belts, scarves
and necklaces on
adhesive hooks.

Keep it fresh:
paint your front door.

Remember where you are.

Always fold sweaters—
hanging stretches

them out.

—Marci Rae Johnson

Freeform

To create freeform found poems, the poet uses a source text
or texts, excerpts words or phrases, and rearranges them to
make a new, original poem.

The Sirens

from Franz Kafka's "Parable and Paradox"

These are the seductive voices
of the night; the Sirens too
sang that way.

It would be doing them an injustice
to think that they wanted
to seduce;

they knew they had claws and sterile
wombs, and they lamented
this aloud.

They could not help it
if their laments sounded so
beautiful.

—Rick Maxson

Cento

For the cento, the poet takes full lines from other poets and arranges them into a new poem. Unlike freeform found poetry, cento always deals with other poems as source texts and keeps original lines intact. This form goes all the way back to ancient Greeks and Romans, who honored their beloved Homer and Virgil by using these poets' lines in their own collage poems. *Cento,* in fact, comes from the Latin word for "patchwork."

Angela Alaimo O'Donnell wrote the following cento by culling lines from her extensive notebook. She credits "Wistan Hugh, John Paul, Edith, Robert Lee, Rainer Maria, Ignaz Franz, St. Kate, and William Blake."

Notebook Cento

O, wear your tribulation like a rose!
Beauty is the visible form of Good.
We are put on earth for a little space,
you should set the world on fire.

Forgive, O Lord, my little jokes on thee—
Holy God, we praise thy name—
and I'll forgive thy great big one on me—
everlasting is thy reign.
The best is yet to come.
Je ne regrette rien.
In the prison of his days
What does a poet do? I praise.

—Angela Alaimo O'Donnell

There's a Poem on the Side of the Building

Annie Dillard captures the spirit of found poetry (really, she should write odes to it!) in this mini manifesto at the beginning of *Mornings Like This: Found Poems…*

> Happy poets who write found poetry go pawing through popular culture like sculptors on trash heaps. They hold and wave aloft usable artifacts and fragments: jingles and ad copy, menus and broadcasts—all objet trouvés, the literary equivalents of Warhol's Campbell's soup cans and Duchamp's bicycle. By entering a found text as a poem, the poet doubles its context. The original meaning remains intact, but now it swings between two poles. The poet adds, or at any rate increases, the element of delight. This is an urban, youthful, ironic, cruising kind of poetry. It serves up whole texts, or interrupted fragments of texts.

Found poems are commonly likened to collages—literary works of art that combine and layer other sources to make a new piece. I also like to think of them as city murals, which is in keeping with Dillard's use of the word "urban." Colorful and exciting, murals make a statement on the sides of buildings and walls by honoring historical people, ideas, and landmarks.

Milwaukee (which, you'll remember from the sestina chapter also hosts the North Point Lighthouse), is home to a number of striking murals—and the numbers continue to grow, especially with the assistance of Wallpapered City, a consulting group that helps curate and install new murals around the city.

A muralist "doubles the context" of their inspiration like a found poet. Reynaldo Hernandez's "Mural of Peace," located on the south side and visible to motorists heading into the city on I-94, incorporates symbols of an eagle, dove, olive branch, and rainbow with a sketch of the world's continents in the background. The vibrant stripes of several nations' flags emanate from the dove's back.

"All of these are positive images of peace and universality," writes Maayan Silver in "A Deeper Look At Milwaukee's South Side 'Mural Of Peace'"—"but if you look more closely, you can see additional layers. If you look at three stripes together, it is one country's flag, but if you go up one stripe, for each group of three, it's another nation's flag."

Hernandez draws upon universal symbols of peace and nationhood, combines them, and deepens their meaning by drawing the viewer into a new perspective.

A more recent mural, installed on the side of the Dye House in the city's historic Third Ward, was painted by the German street artist Andreas von Chrzanowski, who also goes by the name of CASE.

The project is enormous, covering a height of six stories. The mural looks large enough from the highway. Approach it on foot off East Buffalo Street, as I did during an early summer visit to Milwaukee—ice cream in hand—and it positively looms.

According to a press release from Wallpapered City, the painting was intended to "pay homage not only to the women who used to dye nylons there, but to the many women who work in the Historic Third Ward today and to working people everywhere." Using the award-winning Milwaukee chef Karen Bell as a model, CASE painted a photo-realistic mural of Bell, her figure tucked between window sets, on a span of building which is all but windowless at its center (two windows at the very edge of her sleeve flashed at me in the afternoon light; the rest of her figure commanded my vision from an opaque surface).

Looking up at the mural is an exercise in perspective shift. I stood gazing, while she appeared to be sitting on a floating surface, knees bent beneath her—with crossed hands, both gnarled and lithe at once, set lightly on one knee...a white apron the one barrier between her palm and her jeans.

CASE's painting, focusing on the work attire and the hands, indeed pays homage to work. But like a good found poet, the artist has interpreted his source material, Ms. Bell, in a different way. He did not include her head. The collar of her crimson shirt opens at the top of the building, and her head, as it were, disappears into the clouds.

Some residents dislike the mural, claiming the woman deserves a head. Why should the anonymous women who helped build the city continue to go on faceless, with no identity but the work they provided? Others believe the mural pays homage exactly as it should by focusing on the power of women's productive hands. Standing on that hot Milwaukee street, I know I felt a sense of awe and tremendous respect standing in her shadow.

What do both of these murals have in common? They generate thought and conversation beyond merely pulling from outside sources. They create, as Eliot says, "a whole of feeling which is unique, utterly different from that from which it was torn."

My Found Poetry Journey

Found poetry is my go-to cure for writer's block because it gives me some footing in an existing source while still making full demand of my brain. As I've probably made pretty clear by now, found poetry isn't about riding the coattails of other writers. It's about sewing your own coattails using pieces of their fabric. (For the record, I don't actually own any coattails.) However, having a coattail to grab is a big boost to the creative process, better than reaching into thin air.

In my recent journey into freeform found poetry, I wanted to delve deeper into the world of autism. Dan Bowman, a fellow writer, is a close friend of mine who was diagnosed with autism well into adulthood. As he has worked on understanding his diagnosis, I have attempted to learn some things along with him. After reading his series of articles from his "Notes From the Spectrum" series at *Ruminate Magazine* and highlighting words and phrases that cut to the heart, I wrote the following poem.

Notes from the Spectrum

—*found poem based on Daniel Bowman, Jr.'s*
  "Notes from the Spectrum" series at Ruminate Magazine, *2016*

There's no obvious starting point.

The autistic life is alienation,
something rich and strange.
All the pieces form white clouds
I watch in my peripheral.

What moves you?
A single plum tree?
A small boat lost on a vast sea?

Please say things that are true
and beautiful, almost decadent:
boughs heavy with ripe
Osage oranges, the muted glow
of plump bumblebees.
Ride *in* the world, never merely past it.

I blow on my knuckles,
clap between movements,
create disturbances in a world
where every tiny pebble in the road
threatens a crash.

God forbid, touch me.

No one is safe in this world,
but it's all still unfolding.
It is not a matter of *if,* but *how*—

bullfrogs croaking, turkey vultures soaring,
the oddly textured spheres
of fallen fruit.

The poem is one hundred percent Dan's words and one hundred percent my conception of them. How that process works, exactly, is always a bit of a mystery. I went with my instinct at first, choosing words from his articles that struck me. Then I retyped those into a document and moved, grouped, and shifted lines in a way that, well, for the lack of a better term, felt *right.* That's the beauty of found poetry. You and the author of your source text are collaborating, even if you aren't physically together. Dan wouldn't have written that poem himself, but then again, I couldn't have written it without him.

Your Leg of the Trip

The best thing about found poetry is that it's easy to get started. Again, it shouldn't just be an exercise of moving words around but an act of creative engagement and transformation. However, once you get some source material, you have a foundation from which to begin.

Using erasure, cut-up, freeform, or cento, write a found poem. (When time permits, of course, I hope you will try all four.) Since found poetry can go in so many wonderful directions, you may not find step-by-step guidance as helpful as tips to keep in mind:

1. Find source material that is inspiring to you—emphasis on *you*. You may find a spark in the operating instructions for your new air fryer, a letter from a soldier during the Vietnam War, or the poetry of Anne Sexton. *Inspiration* literally means *breath of life,* but life isn't always milkshakes and roses. A source text may fill you with joy, but also anger or confusion. Go with those feelings. And remember, if you are clearly making a new work, and you cite your source, you are okay with fair use. Still nervous or not sure? Use text that falls within the public domain. Some of the best found poetry, in fact, derives from older texts reimagined in a new context.

2. Get organized. As I said, the process can feel gloriously mysterious, but it's still a process. Always make sure you know what source you're using and write that information down in a safe place in case identifying information gets cut up, blacked out, or otherwise lost. Don't underestimate the value of a good highlighter!

3. Make sure your poem can stand on its own. In other words, although you will cite your source, your poem should make sense and shine without it. Having access to the source material may inform and enrich your readers' experience, but they shouldn't have to rely on it to connect with your poem.

10

Haiku in the Spaces Between

When we travel, it might seem to be primarily about the destination—lighthouse, UFO museum, The White River Suspension Bridge. But that misses a big part of any great trip. Lots of memories are made in the mini-van, the RV, the hotel that turned out not to be quite what we hoped it would be.

Haiku knows this, from its very beginnings, where it emerged from social gatherings and travels—parties along the way, fresh insights on the paths there and back.

Originally functioning as an element in a Japanese party-game form (*tanka*, a five-line poem in which a *hokku* provided the opening three lines, capped by a two-line ending), the hokku eventually broke free and set out on its own, becoming the haiku we understand and love.

Tanka was most often written chain style—as a *renga*—with one member of the party providing the first three 5-7-5-syllable lines and another capping it with a transitional two-line 7-7-syllable section that would become the link to another tanka; this would continue, with more party members adding to the chain, in a similar fashion, while the drinks poured freely. Sometimes rowdy, always inviting intellectual challenge, tanka and renga provided a bonding opportunity through collaborative poetry writing.

The Haiku Society of America defines haiku as "a short poem that uses imagistic language to convey the essence of an experience of nature or the season intuitively linked to the human condition." That's a rather formal way to describe what was born through party poetry. And, though, arguably, the haiku form went on to become more "serious" and even, at some level, transcendent, it might surprise some poets to know that the form invites punning, right at its heart.

Because Japanese and English don't quite match up line- and syllable-wise (for one thing, Japanese haiku were written in a single vertical line), it is hard to produce an exact match when carrying the form over. While popular culture has mostly settled on a three-line 5-7-5 syllable pattern, coming to a total of 17 syllables, there's flexibility. This was true of the form even in Japanese, as the great Bashō famously told his followers, "If you have three or four, even five or seven extra syllables, but the poem still sounds good, don't worry about it. But if one syllable stops the tongue, look at it hard."

Here's one of the most famous haiku by Bashō (1644- 1694)—a poet who chose to live as a wanderer, and for whom the road trip, on foot, was always his deepest love:

upon a lifeless branch
crow has descended
autumn nightfall

Carrying it over from Japan, let's follow with a few good English ones, generously provided by my friend Joshua Gage, of previous ghazal fame. Note: they have nothing to do with 5-7-5 (they all have fewer syllables), but everything to do with capturing a moment.

Super bowl
the last wing
in the basket

melting snow
I remember
that I am dust

coffee break
the lulling tempo
of winter rain

—Joshua Gage

Haiku has its own long history in English—inviting, as Jane Hirshfield puts it, a "renewed intensity of perception" where "the brief poem murmurs, 'Just this, just this,' opening the reader to the sharpness of each blade of grass, on whose sword-tip the universe flowers." Experience these, for instance, which also take big liberties with syllable count—and even line count:

an icicle the moon drifting through it

—Matsuo Allard

Nuance

Even the iris bends
When a butterfly lights upon it.

—Amy Lowell

dense fog
a mockingbird
fills it

—Charles B. Dickson

When I met Christopher Patchel, another great American haiku writer, I was still in 5-7-5 mode, and this was after earning two degrees in creative writing. (I tell you, what we learn in second grade has a way of persisting!) After spending some time with him and his writing, I started to learn more about the spirit of haiku and was amazed at what I had been missing.

Patchel describes his own personal experience with the form as...

a eureka discovery for me [that] had nothing to do with syllable count but rather the poetic power of so few words, the alchemy of its techniques and aesthetics. The immediacy of sensory images (the ultimate in *show, don't tell*), a sense of time and eternity with a focus on present experience against the backdrop of

perennial seasons, the juxtaposition and disjunction
of images (most haiku are split into two parts).

Here are some of Patchel's haiku:

slant light…
to each leaf
its own fall

a path of leaves
our conversation
turns wordless

used books
I leave the shop
an hour older

—Christopher Patchel

So if a haiku is not primarily about 5-7-5, how do you go about
writing one? What should it focus on?

Patchel brings up a few key elements we can include in
our mental checklist:

Immediacy: Capture a moment.
Sensory images: Show, don't tell, something about the
natural world through the senses.
Seasons: Include a *kijo,* or a word that reflects a season.
Juxtaposition: include a *kireji,* or pivot, that contrasts two

parts of the haiku. This could be a cutting word, or phrase, or punctuation—such as a dash or ellipses—that conveys a shift. (This, by the way, is where the poet is invited to pun; the kireji then literally pivots on a linguistic turnstile!)

Let's take another look at one of Patchel's haiku and see how some of these elements come into play:

slant light...
to each leaf
its own fall

Immediacy: We have a leaf falling in light, not an abstract concept of time.

Sensory images: Light and leaves. I can see the leaf fall and feel that mild warmth of low autumn sunlight.

Seasons: The kijo here is "fall." While the word is referring to the action, not the literal season, it does the job (along with a play on words).

Juxtaposition: The haiku pivots after the first line, contrasting the life of light and the death of falling. And, whether or not Patchel meant "leaf" as a pun, it can serve as one, calling to mind both the leaf itself and the act of leaving.

If it seems you have to remember a lot to compose such a small poem, just remind yourself of the sestina's long climb. Forms take time and going the distance. With the long practice of haiku, you'll find that its essential elements tend to eventually come as flashes of insight.

Don't Let Those Haiku Slip By

When it comes to the journey of writing in form, a haiku could almost be thought of as a painting in a local gallery or a postcard of a destination—an image caught in time.

But even that doesn't seem quite right. Paintings and postcards almost feel too expansive, too permanent.

Again, from Joshua Gage, who actually builds on both the Shintoism roots (all things have aliveness!) and Buddhist roots (all is impermanence!) of haiku:

> Haiku are a moment, a breath. If we're using travel as a metaphor, it's a single pigeon in a Venice street that looks at you funny, or the coolness of fresh sheets after you've marched around the Grand Canyon all day. Haiku are literally the moments in between, those brief bursts and pauses that catch your attention and focus for just a second then disappear. They are much more ephemeral and fleeting than a painting or similar object.

A picture may capture a memory of your travels, but nothing compares to the experienced moment itself. The split second in mid-air above cherry blossoms while spinning on the carnival ride, the spray of water in your face while standing on the suspension bridge, the glimpse of a blackbird in the cattails as you enter the roundabout.

Haiku are not a mode of travel, roadside attraction, or even a depiction of such. They are the vibrant spaces between.

My Haiku Journey

It's true that sestinas, villanelles, rondeaux and the like are challenging. They're complex, downright fussy forms. Still, I dive into them knowing that with so many words and poetic devices at my disposal, I can somehow make them work, even learn about myself in the process. And that's pretty much what happens.

But haiku requires presence. Full engagement with moments. And I don't always like to take the time to do that.

National Haiku Writing Month, otherwise known as NaHaiWriMo, challenges poets to write one haiku per day during the month of February (the shortest month, appropriately). A couple of years ago, I decided to take on the challenge, though I held off until April, probably because I was too busy sorting my conversation candy hearts.

Haiku are short and sweet, of course, so when I had a month of haiku-writing ahead of me, I felt pretty calm at first. *I'll write when I take a walk,* I thought. *Or when I drive to the store or do my spring cleaning. This is something I can do!* But every time I thought about writing haiku, I found reason to distract myself with music, talking, or writing Facebook messages, to-do lists, articles—any expressive activity I could enter and exit seamlessly with some semblance of control.

The aforementioned Josh Gage took interest in my interest, though, and sent me postcards of haiku he wrote in February. He also sent me two books, *Haiku: A Poet's Guide,* by Lee Gurga, and *The Haiku Handbook,* by William Higginson. I dove into these books but froze up the moment I thought about writing. Josh told me I was thinking too hard.

I've always considered myself to be more of a feeler than a thinker. (I'm close to 100% *F* on the Myers-Briggs test.) But my tendency to *think* rather than *be* reared its cerebral head during my own haiku month, when the notion of opening myself up to so many crystallized, living moments set me on edge.

Eventually, though, because I knew I'd made a commitment, I had to write *something*. So during one the coldest, snowiest Midwestern springs on record, I sought out, wherever I could, imagistic moments that conveyed the human condition. I approached those times of seeking with much more trepidation than I did for sestinas or even my airplane villanelles, wherein I challenged myself to complete cogent drafts during short flights. Three short lines composed of juxtaposed images proved to ask more attention than I was willing, or wanting, to give. In the end, I wrote about ten haiku.

Before my haiku month started, I had anticipated writing maybe, oh, a hundred. We're talking just two or three lines a pop. But I stalled out. Maybe I was, indeed, overthinking. Or maybe I was busier than usual. Or maybe I just needed more practice.

The results didn't necessarily make me want to burn my poetry degrees. In fact, I got a few good haiku out of the experience:

spring snow—
the daffodils
hang their heads

foreclosure—
robin perched
in the rafters

spring cleaning—
dust clings to her ponytail

I know that what I need the most practice with is *noticing. Being. Presence. Encounter.* All that "living in the moment" stuff that gets such rave reviews. And although I wish I had come up with more haiku during that month, poems exist now that didn't before. My journey is just beginning.

Your Leg of the Trip

As we wind down our form-poem travels, I want to do something a bit different. For your assignment, I'd rather you create a long-term habit rather than complete an exercise.

Whether you're using this book in a class or going about form poetry on your own, I encourage you to cultivate the daily practice of reading or writing haiku. That's right, one haiku per day. Perhaps you'll read or write a haiku every day of the semester, or month, or week. Better yet, you could go a year or beyond. Maybe it could become a permanent part of your daily life, like brushing your teeth. (If you don't brush your teeth every day, I don't want to know.) The key is consistency. As one who has gone through waves of reading and not reading, writing and not writing haiku, I can attest to the vitality of keeping at it.

So how do you form the haiku habit?

Remember connecting footsteps to sonnets? Writer Rose Caiola "embraces the haiku moment," as well, by taking walks. First, she releases her worries and concerns, "Then I breathe, let go, and bring my mind to a place of calm, ready to observe and be part of the moment unfolding before me. The haiku come out of this moment. I gaze out my window, breathe a few long, cleansing breaths, and start writing." You could take a similar stance if getting ready to simply read haiku.

Sometimes Caiola composes a complete haiku in the moment; other times, she records images or fragments and turns them into haiku later. Despite all these references to presence and breath and encounter, there's nothing wrong with *working* on haiku. Crafting, polishing, and revising is part of the experience, not a detraction. The moment itself, though, the feeling you embody with your haiku, is an ephemeral experience.

Walks are wonderful for the body and soul, but sometimes they don't happen every day. How can you create other opportunities for "haiku moments"?

- Look up from your work (or your phone) for a moment to gaze out the window
- Take in your surroundings while waiting at a red light
- Turn even brief moments outdoors into "haiku moments"—taking out the trash, checking the mail, entering the grocery store. You don't have to be camping in a national park to interact with the natural world

However you enter the moment, breathe and be. Encounter

the aliveness right in front of you, no matter how subtle. Let yourself **go Bashō.** He ultimately took for his model of haiku the "artless expression of a child at play." And he went with it.

~

Go the Extra Mile (Try Haibun)

Haibun is a combination of alternating sections of prose and haiku, usually in the form of an autobiographical diary or travelogue, though it can also be a description of a place, person, or object; an essay; or even a short story.

The form was popularized by Bashō. He wrote many travelogues, combining verse and prose into a poetic diary about his journeys—mostly on foot—visiting all the places mentioned in the verses of Saigyō (a poet whose work he greatly admired), as well as shrines, mountains, and Japan's islands. On these journeys, he traveled with friends, visited friends, or trekked alone. His most famous haibun is *Oku no Hosomichi* (*The Narrow Road to the Deep North* or *The Narrow Road to the Interior*). Ultimately, we see that for Bashō the road was not just a background; it embodied Zen, poetry, and life itself.

Turning our attention to English haibun, here is a sample from poet Michelle Ortega:

Let the Questions Go Unanswered

Elizabeth Street Garden, SoHo, NYC.

A Sphinx, headdress and breastplate of a warrior, guards the garden. It's 82° in October; my daughter and I have no wisdom for the riddle, but she allows us to pass.

Vines climb nearby buildings, remind us of a cemetery in Paris. Roses strain toward the sun, bees fervent over Echinacea, tiny pineapples sprout in metal urns. An iguana with a turquoise collar suns on the back of a stone lion, its thin leash drops to the owner on a bench below.

Old-bookstore scents blend with turning leaves and over-ripe butterfly bushes. The statue of a Grecian woman rises amid the SoHo backdrop:

> delicate concrete,
> one bare breast—
> her dress pressed by a breeze

—Michelle Ortega

Now, your turn.

Set out to create a haibun. For a shorter haibun, try one paragraph of prose followed by one haiku. For something this brief, try to stick to a single place, time, or incident. Both the prose section *and* the haiku should add their own meaning, so the combined piece will say more than either part could alone.

Switchbacks: Finding the Right Form for Your Poem

I'm a firm believer in form sparking creativity, not hindering it. By setting limits, form taps into previously undiscovered stores of inspiration, releasing poems you didn't know were there. My hope is that the journeys of these forms have brought you to fresh and surprising destinations.

But what about those times when you know *what* you want to write about, but you're just not sure *how?* What if instead of discovering your subject through form, you want to find the best form for your subject?

Whatever you want to write about, there's a form for that.

In the "Form It" series at Tweetspeak Poetry, L.L.Barkat recommends choosing a form that either "matches or purposely works against how you feel as you approach your topic, or that matches or purposely works against the nature of the topic itself."

For example, let's say you want to write about the nagging persistence of a migraine. The spiraling, obsessive nature of a sestina may match the nature of a migraine, while an ode, which usually celebrates its subject, may work against it. Try both and see what new ideas come to light. Or let's say you finally want to share a lifelong secret, say, a love for those puffy orange circus peanut candies. Do you reveal it through the more mysterious acrostic, or sing it from the rooftop of an in-your-face form such as the villanelle?

Ezra Pound famously revised his "In a Station of the Metro" from 30 lines down to the haiku-like poem we know today:

In a Station of the Metro

The apparition of these faces in the crowd;
Petals on a wet, black bough.

To capture his sudden vision of humanity on the train platform, he had to get it down to only two lines. The subject needed the form. It's hard to imagine this poem any other way.

While most forms cannot be limited to just a few purposes—there's rarely an easy, fill-in-the-blank choice—they do complement certain moods and occasions. Think of the following list as a "quick guide" to some common uses and characteristics of the forms we've studied.

Villanelle: useful for exploring cycles or themes that feel resistant to answers; can also be used to work against a topic, using mocking humor

Sonnet: excellent way to confine or rein in a potentially sappy, bombastic, or overly sentimental theme; also an excellent way to work against a topic humorously

Sestina: good for exploring confusion, questions, worries, obsessions, neuroses, and fears in an oblique way

Acrostic: good for showing and hiding, making a subversive comment or observation

Ghazal: helpful for emphasizing longing or for exploring metaphysical questions

Pantoum: useful for plumbing memory and exploring the past

Ode: excellent way to praise something or someone you love or admire

Rondeau: helpful for giving form to extremes of either sadness or dark wit, commemorating an event, or singing to someone or something

Found poem: helpful for exploring a variety of voices and generating new thoughts and perspectives on a subject

Haiku: good for creating immediacy or focusing in on an emotion or encounter

More Stops

Examples and Prompts to Inspire
Your Journey

Villanelles

To My Mother

I held you captive in my sight
while evil fingers burrowed deep.
I heard you crying in the night.

While you focused on the light
and pumpkin-apple deer stood watch
I held you captive in my sight.

You pulled strings, made magic sleight
with finger-writing in the air.
I heard you crying in the night.

I gathered words and tried to write
of memories and times gone by
to hold you captive in my sight.

Your body spent, the timing right
and just before the snow fell soft,
I heard you silent in the night.

You transcribed life and fought the fight
then shook and snapped the earthly chains
that held you captive in my sight.
I hear you laughing in the night.

Sandra Heska King

Prompt: Write a villanelle addressed to another person. When choosing your refrains, think about what you want to communicate to your audience and how the repetition will intensify your tone. Are you pleading? Making a declaration? Employing irony?

Summer Conditioning

RUN!
The coach said.
Like you mean it!

The fun
streams down your forehead,
running

past your tongue,
bitten so it won't spread
what you mean. It

has already begun:
the shame-red
run

away from shunning.
The fear led
you to mean it.

And with abandoned passion
you bow your head.
Run
like you mean it.

Todd C. Truffin

Prompt: Write a villanelle in which you choose two very short refrains—no more than a few words long. Like Truffin, challenge yourself to make at least one of the refrains a single word. Note that while his center lines rhyme, his refrains do not. How does that variation add to (or detract from) the poem's meaning? I'll leave the choice of whether to rhyme your refrains up to you.

Science Fiction

Last night, we watched the moon turn dark,
drank Rolling Rock on cobblestones. Little airplanes
fumbled through the clouds, eager for a look

at the eclipse. How carbon-based we are,
hair, some bone, mostly water. Small, plain,
last night, when we watched the moon turn dark

as morning on I-64: residents of the horse park
robed in mist like coddled bishops, their heads craned,
fumbling through the fog to sneak a look

at my Japanese death trap speeding to work.
And over this hill is another hill. The wax, the wane.
But last night, as we watched the moon turn dark,

I twitched, dumb-eyed, convinced some residual spark
might lift us over roof and brick. Of course we stayed
grounded: fumbling, human, dying for one quick look.

Luminous beings are we, not this crude matter—
lovely to believe, but this morning we are the same
as last night, when we watched the moon turn dark
and we gaped through the clouds, aching for a look.

Erin Keane

Prompt: In "Science Fiction," Keane varies her refrains, particularly the second one, progressively. Watch how the diction,
and resulting overall tone, changes:

fumbled through the clouds, eager for a look
fumbling through the fog to sneak a look

grounded: fumbling, human, dying for one quick look.
and we gaped through the clouds, aching for a look.

Write a villanelle in which one or both refrains evolves. When does a variation become "too much"? How do these changes impact the poem as a whole? These are vital questions for poets to ask.

Echo

I couldn't understand the thing he told me.
He said he couldn't make it any clearer:
I'd rather die of thirst than have you hold me.

Hold me, I said. His elegance consoled me,
and his refusal made him all the dearer.
I couldn't understand. The thing he told me,

twice (how could anyone repeat it?), bowled me
over. I put it to myself, and queerer:
I'd rather die of thirst than have you hold me?

Just look at me at least, I wished. Behold me!
You wish, he mocked and looked toward his mirror.
I couldn't understand the thing he told me.

Perhaps our likenesses, not love, controlled me.
Then something turned and spoke in me. I hear her:
I'd rather die of thirst then have you hold me

is what I should have said to draw him nearer.
We have in common our redundant error.
I couldn't understand the thing he told me:
I'd rather die of thirst than have you hold me.

John Poch

Prompt: In this villanelle, poet John Poch explores the mytho-
logical story of Echo and Narcissus. Write your own villanelle
in the voice of a character from mythology, religion, literature,
or television/film.

At the Window

I look at you, as if
for the first time, purpled
against the fading gift

of day. I gingerly lift
the glass, decades-rippled
and I look at you, as if

these years had not a rift
between you and me created
against the fading gift

of fragrance, lilac shrift
upon the wind unstated
and I look at you, as if

for the first time adrift
on the wind, unrelated,
and I look at you as if
against a fading gift.

L.L. Barkat

Prompt: Poet L.L. Barkat varies the villanelle form by removing a stanza, keeping the poem to sixteen lines. How does the shorter length speak to the subject matter and themes? Write a villanelle that has fewer, or more, than nineteen lines.

Sonnets

That New

At the market today, I look for Piñata
apples, their soft-blush-yellow. My husband
brought them home last week, made me guess at
the name of this new strain, held one in his hand
like a gift and laughed as I tried all
the names I knew: Gala, Fuji, Honey

Crisp—watched his face for clues—what to call
something new? It's winter, only tawny
hues and frozen ground, but that apple bride
was sweet, and I want to bring it back to him,
that new. When he cut it, the star inside
held seeds of other stars, the way within
a life are all the lives you might live,
each unnamed, until you name it.

Susan Rothbard

Prompt: In "That New," Rothbard travels from present to past, and present to past again, using the visual cue and memory of an apple. The final couplet has only the barest echo of a rhyme (*live* and *it*). Do you think the poet made that choice for any reason besides being unable to find a final rhyme? (Poets can always find rhymes, right?) How does the choice potentially enhance the poem's movement between past and present, named and unnamed? Write a sonnet in which you "time travel" with the help of a central image. Use the couplet to emphasize the connection (or disconnection) of the times you're traveling between.

(Note: poem below wraps to indent on one long line)

Sonnet (With Children)

My love is like a deep and placid lake...
Not now, sweetie, Daddy's busy, OK?

OK: my love's a deep and peaceful lake...
Here, Daddy can fix it. All better. Now go play.
Um, my love, yes—a rose that blooms in spring...
You tell her Daddy says she has to share.
My love's...My love's a lake that blooms—no, that springs...
On the wall?! Her what?! No, wait—I'll be right there.
OK—love, lake, spring, joy, flower bedding...
And why is the house so quiet now, I wonder?
Ah, fuck it! (Whoops! Don't say that!) You know where
    I'm heading.
Don't touch a thing—I need to get the plunger!
Forgive me, love, but time, as you know, is ticking.
So here: no you, no joy, no life. No kidding.

Gabriel Spera

Prompt: Take a turn at writing a surprising or humorous sonnet, using some of the techniques Spera employs in "Sonnet (With Children)"—contrasts, dialogue, punctuation, parenthetical expressions, interjections—to keep your reader on the move.

When the Eye and the Ear and the Voice

have been exhausted by the constant screens,
click—screens—scroll—news feeds of worry—noises—
thudding through the sternum—nothing unseen;
when wounded eyes, stuffed ears, ranted voices

appear—with particular static—in dreams
that once held the beloved and her choice
word, his scarred cheek—breaking news—no serene
sight, no song, no throated pleasure to voice—

from a man's hands, three wordless chords descend,
a woman draws with a bow a sharp light
from autumn's intimate dusk. Breathe. Repent.
Unclench your fist, supplicant. When the eye

the ear, the voice disappear, then atone.
Now, silence. Then, again, a voice to begin.

David Wright

Prompt: Similar to Spera's poem "Sonnet (With Children),"
Wright's poem uses punctuation to particular effect. The constant interruption of the dashes helps communicate the foiled
building up of constancy in love. By the third stanza, the
punctuation shifts, and hope is born. This is the chance for
renewal. Write a sonnet in which your punctuation creates a
clear effect for the first half of the poem; then shift your
punctuation choices to create a new effect that either grows
out of or agitates against the effect in the first half of the
poem.

A Sonnet for the Architect

—for Andi

The site has been selected, so they dig,
to break in soft and untouched grass. So draw
the plan. Then draw again. You lay your wrist,
poor broken wrist near mine, so red, and all
among my pens and paper you—stopping—
glance over metaphors and images
to find that all my iambs were blocking
your compass. Circles erase blemishes;
lend more, more of your protracted scratches
to build a roof. Not build, exactly. To
pitch for us some meaning, and me thatched. It's
for you, the desk, the translucent bright blue
paper. I use mine to make a bandage
for your wrist; you yours to draw the landing.

Isaac Willis

Prompt: Write a sonnet addressed directly to another person.
If you completed the similar prompt with the villanelle (see
Sandra Heska King's "To My Mother"), consider the difference in using these two forms as a mean of address. When
might a villanelle be more effective? When might a sonnet?

The Creation

was going well. A perfect, rosy sow,
a finch, an elephant. Then a giraffe
at the last minute, sprang up like Wow,
an exclamation point on legs. A gaffe.
or maybe not.
      Her fringy eyelashes,
her voice, a bleat soft as a low laugh,
a yard-long black tongue to lick and catch
leaves from the sky. She nuzzles her newborn calf,
still wet, eyes shut, legs splayed and sliding,
the two of them improbable sweet chaff
of the imagination, hang-gliding
off the cliff of reason.
      Oh giraffes,
gather around, bend down your horns. Remind me,
when all seems dark and sane, of mystery.

Jeanne Murray Walker

Prompt: Like an ode, the sonnet "The Creation" praises an object of wonder with vivid, sensory detail. Write a sonnet of celebration that includes as many senses as possible while adhering to the Shakespearean sonnet form.

Sestinas

The Muse

Calliope, when she packed up and came
to Oklahoma, first went out and found
a calico white cotton dress, two out-
side baggy pockets on the front for stuffing tangled
wild onion stocks she gathered from the hills.
She hummed a bit and tried to look less holy.

On Sunday she would belt the hymns with holy-
rollers. They told her they were glad she came.
That's where she met Hank Smith, who lived among the hills
of rusted junk outside of town. They found
a lot to talk about. He liked to comb her tangled
blonde hair and pick the burs and grass bits out.

When folks would ask about her past, her outside life, he told them to shove off and holy
shit, now what man could care how tangled
up her dim past might be, when she just came
in from the evening rain, bright as a penny found
inside the pocket of some fresh washed jeans. The hills

bore silent witness of their love, the way the hills
will do. But from his lips the muse called out
a song to make the rusted car parts holy
when morning sun greased down the heaps. He found

himself much lighter since she came,
his thoughts, like clear-burned field, less tangled.

The morning that she found the doe, all tangled
in fencing strung around the rusting hills,
he held her while she cried and later came
to her when tears had wrung her out
and offered up himself to be hers wholly.
And after that entanglement they found

they could not bear to part. The ladies found,
concerned about her absence from the church, them tangled
in knots of naked arms and legs and wholly
unbothered by the knocks that echoed from the hills.
But later on the scrap-man's boy called out
for Hank, and just his weathered hound dog came.

They found him wandering through the hills, his eyes
wrung out: what came from getting tangled up
with all that holy, holy, holy.

Benjamin Myers

Prompt: In "The Muse," Myers uses the sestina form with the unusual purpose of telling a story. Write a sestina that follows a narrative: beginning, middle, and end.

Sestina to Bind a Goodbye

When morning rose on the old blue car
parked in front of the shingled house,
the people inside were already up: the father
making coffee for the road, the mother
at the table, trying to wrap a globe,
and the daughter, combing out her knots.

The father, too, was thinking of knots,
his job to tie to the top of the car
the overflow of stuff. He eyed the globe.
"Are we going to clean out the *house*?"
he said. Testy today, the mother
thought, but said, "She *asked*—" and the father

sighed a sigh that said, of all the father
tasks—tying, untying, retying knots—
you are the one most tedious. The mother
figured what're hard are ends, and said, "In my car,
in the trunk, is rope," and just as the house
caught a sliver of light, turned back to her globe.

How do you wrap/pack a spinnable globe?
Box? Garbage bag? "Just toss it," the father
said, "in the car." She gave him a look; the house
gave off its morning creak. "This rope's a snarl of knots,"
he said. The girl began taking loads to the car,
filling the seats and trunk. The mother's

solution for the globe? Mummify with towels—*her* mother's
towels; *then* the bag, then the tape, is how to pack a globe.
Pleased and all ceremonious, she carried it to the car
where, cinching its half-hitches tight, the father
said of the overflow, "This puppy's not
going *any*where!" The thrill of loss hung over the house,

the gabled, peeling, spiderwebbed house,
but too, the thrill of finding. "Bye," said the mother,
"I love you, call," and fingered the father's suspect knot.
Wasn't it just a *little* loose around the mummified globe?
"The coffee! Wait, *wait,* hold on, yelled the father,
dashing back, as the girl—va-*rooomm*—starts up the car.

From the house, now less one spinnable globe,
the mother cried, "Check…" and the father,
"…the knots!" to the pulling-away blue car.

Murray Silverstein

Prompt: In "Sestina to Bind a Goodbye," Silverstein captures
family dynamics by choosing mostly domestic teleutons and
incorporating dialogue into every stanza but the first. The use
of "mother" and "father," in particular, naturally positions the
poem to examine relationships. Write a sestina that explores a
relationship or multiple relationships with its choice of teleutons and natural dialogue.

(Note: long-line poem below wraps to indents)

The Proposal

"Perhaps, let's go to Delft, "
he said, taking the silver tea caddy
gingerly off the shelf. It was Betjeman and Barton—
not the shelf, which was of rosewood,
but the caddy painted slight with numbers, *avoirdupois,*
the weight of tea I steep to pour in porcelain.

"Why should we?" I lifted porcelain.
Not the kind they make in Delft—
copied from the Chinese, high-resistance, unlike the
    measure *avoirdupois*
adopted through a confluence of words…Latin, French
    as the tea caddy
I opened for the promise, that petaled-rose would
spread its fragrance with Darjeeling; Betjeman and Barton

sell it so. I wonder if it's Betjeman or Barton
who dreamed of almonds, grapes and peonies to drift in
    porcelain.
Who bare-suggested in a whisper that a hint of rose would
be a better choice than, let's just say, a tulip, yellow, plucked
    from Delft?
I mused on Netherland's canals and stretched towards the
    tea caddy.
What if he could weigh my thoughts in dark *avoirdupois?*

A measure partly from the Latin, *avoirdupois*
came over from *to have, to hold, possess,* like the Betjeman and
    Barton
I hold this very moment, twisting cover of a tight-sealed
    tea caddy
which, had it come from long ago, might rather be of bone-
    ash porcelain
hand-painted blue with scenes of domesticity from Delft.
Milk maids, windmills, a tulip—not a rose—would

play across it like the Madagascar sun on rosewood
stolen from the tropics, shipped through China, measured
    in *avoirdupois*—
all multiples of which are based on pounds, like stones of
    city walls in Delft.
You cannot find this in the catalog from Betjeman and
    Barton,
the knowledge that the British added stones as hard as
    fired porcelain,
or that the city once exploded like the fragrance from this
    silver tea caddy,

assaulting air and narrow streets with powder they don't
    sell in tea caddies,
brass-mounted, inlaid carefully, satin-wood or rosewood,
the larger ones called tea chests, often seated near the
    porcelain
in dining rooms where merchandise bears not the paint
    of bold *avoirdupois*
but is quite fragrant with rare teas of fine purveyors. Bet-

jeman and Barton
is my favorite, see, residing in the heart of passion—
    Paris—not in Delft.

I place the silver tea caddy directly on the shelf, unpainted
    with the weight of ebony *avoirdupois,*
silver tipped with fresh-spilled leaves scattered on the
    rosewood, lined with Betjeman and Barton
rarities to pour into my porcelain, which would, I tell him,
    never come from Delft.

L.L. Barkat

Prompt: "The Proposal" was playfully written in answer to a challenge from poet James Cummins, who handed Barkat the six teleutons one early morning, via email. The end-words seemed disparate, but, in fact, some of them were related to historic ways of handling tea. Even the mind-boggling word *avoirdupois* stepped out of history, being a long-ago measure of weight. Write a sestina that gathers its six end-words from an industry with a history: bookmaking; clothmaking; the crafting of timepieces, instruments, or jewelry; or some other historical business. Do a little research and choose your end-words from what you discover. Teach the reader something along the way, but make it seem like play.

(Note: long-line poem below wraps to indents)

Harriette Winslow and Aunt Rachel Clean Collard Greens on Prime Time Television

In their dollhouse kitchen,
they clean a bouquet
of collards
while the comedy of errors
unfolds around them—
Harriette in her pantsuit and that blackmother

smirk that signals the hard love only a mother
can muster. This, holy kitchen,
culinary sanctuary, covers them
in light, its white glory a bouquet
around their perfect hair. Their fingers know no errors
as they pick and place the collards.

There was an earthy magic in my mother cleaning collards,
their mineral scent, the sink-full of water my mother
plunged them into, the water which washed them of their
    errors—
greens baptized, clean from sediment and rock, our kitchen
sink her pulpit, the leafy bouquet
her holy book. How we wished we could be them,

touched by our mother's godly hands, then
cleaned so well we forgot they were just collards—
they glistened, a sparkling bouquet
of dinner-yet-to-come, so loved by our mother

that even they forgot their natural bitterness. A kitchen
is sweetened when collards are cooking, the air a

swelling porkfat perfume, the onion's pungent terror
nulled by the ribboned greens—I loved to watch my mother
    cut them,
roll the piles of flat foliage up like a cigar, the kitchen
knife shining against a tight army of collards.
We needed no superheroes when we had her, a mother
to rival every black mom on cable—no fragrant bouquet

could rival the smell of her greens and cornbread, the
    bouquet
of cotton swabs and peroxide she'd use to sanitize our
    playground errors.
She was a magician, more than just another mother—
she could turn an afro into a constellation of braids, adorn
    them
with a galaxy of beads. She could turn a sprawling batch
    of collards
into a smooth and savory feast, a world exploding in her
    small kitchen.

Someday, mother, I will inherit that sweet bouquet
of cocoa butter, Blue Magic, kitchen smoke and calm night
    air,
the perfume of black motherhood. One day, I will learn
    how to cook them collards.

Ashley M. Jones

Prompt: While the title of the sestina suggests that this poem will be "about" two characters from the 1990s sitcom *Family Matters,* it spirals out into a very personal meditation on the sights, scents, and tastes of motherhood and ends with the speaker's declaration to keep the cycle of collards going. Write a sestina that moves from the outside in, whether you start with a TV show, line from a book, or current event.

Acrostics

What It Feels Like

Part of it simmers barely beneath
superficial, like a sunburn
just under the skin—

A spiritual neuralgia
traveling with time,
following the nerve paths,

Insisting on outlining the nervous
system's most sensitive branches—
down the quadriceps or

Niche where the wings would be—
prickly tingling signaling the brain
to think of the dove that flies away.

Monica Sharman

Prompt: Poet Monica Sharman starts each stanza with a capital letter to spell out the word "PAIN." In a way, this kind of acrostic is "more hidden" than one that puts its message letters at the beginning of each and every line. How does this more subtle use of acrostic inform and complement the meaning of the poem? Now write your own acrostic that uses this same technique.

Crepuscule

Dim half light, the orchard
exhaling its last breath, as
evening makes all colors equal—
reds, blues, greens, now shades of gray.
And here come the deer
tiptoeing down the trail, hesitant,
tentative, ready to bolt, flick their
white tails, disappear
in the hedgerow. This is summer's end,
leaves flaring red and gold, and the garden
is dwindling, as days
grow shorter. Whose name do we
hear in the slow tones the owl calls
to its mate in the thickening dusk?

Barbara Crooker

Prompt: Poet Barbara Crooker uses a subdued form to underscore a subdued, "tentative," yet powerfully beautiful scene. Write your own acrostic in which the letters spell out your picture of an understated experience.

asking me to pause

asking me to pause
quietly on the sidewalk
unassuming, unexpected
I look up
curiously
kindly,
keeping love in play, you
initiate a
sweet
swipe of lips

deb y felio

Prompt: This acrostic hides the small, sweet secret of a surprise kiss. Write a tiny acrostic that likewise captures a tiny (but poem-worthy) moment.

(Note: long-line poem below wraps to indents)

To Be a Fisherman or a Father, You Must

Observe the wonders as they occur around you.
Do not claim them. Feel the artistry
moving through, and be silent.

—Rumi, from "Body Intelligence"

Know that inside the glistening bodies of fish, within secret
Envelopes wonder compels us to tear open, there lie, like
    ore,
Vast stretches of empty hours, mined from our lives, time
Invested in the pursuit of mere existence, of letting our own
Natural radiance loose, and nothing more, and nothing less.
And so you float upon the heavens-heavy surface of the
    water,
Looking at neither side of the reflection, but rather at your
    own
Inner burning, from which a new kind of love is being
    forged.
Like starlight, having traversed centuries to catch your son's
Attention while he studies his own window of night, your
    soul,
Keeping time with breath, also travels between the living
And the lost, between life's riddles and its blessings. You see,

Nothing depends on the catch. Rather, true wisdom is
    rooted
In casting yourself into the growing grandeur of this new
    love.

Faisal Mohyuddin

Prompt: In "To Be a Fisherman or a Father, You Must," Mohyuddin honors and advises a new father while spelling out the name of the infant son, developing and sustaining a theme. It's a sophisticated variation on the grade-school name poems we talked about earlier in the book. It's your turn to write a name acrostic, and go beyond describing someone with just a catalog of adjectives.

(Note: poem below wraps to indent on the last long line)

A Valentine

For her this rhyme is penned, whose luminous eyes,
    Brightly expressive as the twins of Lœda,
Shall find her own sweet name, that nestling lies
    Upon the page, enwrapped from every reader.
Search narrowly the lines!—they hold a treasure
    Divine—a talisman—an amulet
That must be worn *at heart*. Search well the measure—
    The words—the syllables! Do not forget
The trivialest point, or you may lose your labor
    And yet there is in this no Gordian knot

Which one might not undo without a sabre,
    If one could merely comprehend the plot.
Enwritten upon the leaf where now are peering
    Eyes scintillating soul, there lie *perdus*
Three eloquent words oft uttered in the hearing
    Of poets, by poets—as the name is a poet's, too,
Its letters, although naturally lying
    Like the knight Pinto—Mendez Ferdinando—
Still form a synonym for Truth—Cease trying!
    You will not read the riddle, though you do the best
        you *can* do.

Edgar Allan Poe

Prompt: Can you find the pattern that spells out Poe's Valentine's name? (Hint: think of ascending numbers.) Write your own acrostic that spells out a secret person's name, whether that person be an object of your affection, frustration, or curiosity. Rather than use the first letter of each line or stanza, however, try a different approach—the ends of lines, the middles (with strategic spacing, perhaps, so your reader isn't completely at a loss), or locations following an equation or pattern.

Ghazals

(Note: long-line poem below wraps to indents)

Ghazal

Drums sounding from dream-depths, I sleep to keep safe
this city,
to keep dreaming I haven't yet feared death, felt the loss
of this city.

And waking, ever-present dustlight coming through the
screen,
I hear the interminable sound of resounding guns across
this city.

I dress as the gun-sounds grow, the curtains playing with
the breeze
as if shot by a thousand unseen bullets, filled with the
silence of this city.

Outside, the yard is empty, the walls shudder from the
    waves bullet-sounds
make, and for hours I pray, weighing the delicate balance
    in this city.

And when the rotors cease their beating, shells scattered
    across asphalt,
I emerge from the comfort of walls and think I have escaped
    this city.

From the rooftop, turning and hearing a city's death rattle,
    I see
the palace billowing, imagine the president conceding his
    city.

His loss is nothing like his people's—the bricks burned
    and branches broken
over pavement, mothers leading their daughters away from
    this place, this city.

And the smoke from the palace signals to me: I am no
    longer Haroun
but Aaron, marked for earth-wandering, searching for a
    way back to this city.

Battle of N'Djamena - February 2, 2008

Aaron Brown

Prompt: Aaron Brown uses alliteration in the lines of his ghazal to develop a sense of connection between the otherwise non-connected parts, thus creating a feeling of inevitability. It is a story told in chronological order, even if each part of the ghazal can still be read on its own. Write a ghazal that tells a chronological story, and consider using repeating alliteration to hold it together.

(Note: long-line poem below wraps to indents)

Ghazal: Back Home
for Syria, September 2013

Tonight a little boy couldn't walk on water or row back
    home.
The sea turned its old face away. Again, there was a *no, no,*
    back home.

Bahr is how we were taught to measure poetry,
bahr is how we've stopped trying to measure sorrow, back
    home.

"All that blue is the sea, and it gives life, gives life," says
    God to the boy
standing wet at heaven's gate—does he want to return, to
    go back home?

My friend who hates cooking has made that eggplant dish,
says nothing was better than yogurt and garlic and tomato,
    back home.

On the train tracks, a man shouts, "Hold me, hold me," to
    his wife,
bites her sleeve, as if he were trying to tow back home.

Thirteen-year-old Kinan with the big eyes says, "We don't
    want to stay in Europe."
"Just stop the war," he repeats, as if praying, *Grow, grow
    back, home.*

Habibi, I never thought our children would write HELP
    US on cardboard.
Let's try to remember how we met years ago, back home.

On our honeymoon we kissed by the sea, watched it
rock the lights, the fishing boats to and fro, back home.

Zeina Hashem Beck

[*Bahr* is Arabic for "sea" but means "meter" when applied
to poetry.]

Prompt: Zeina Hashim Beck covers terrible subjects through
a collection of mostly mundane situations, with many indi-
viduals asking questions or making remarks. Write a ghazal

that includes a number of scenes, with characters in it who each have something to say, or ask.

(Note: long-line poem below wraps to indents)

The Ancient Dance: A Ghazal

I.

I received birth, grasped this world, and knew deeply that
    it is not enough to view dance,
So I begged, teach me the eons past, I will receive that,
    too. Let me speak through dance.

II.

Kings, sages, mendicants, and, yes, yes, goddesses, all told
    with my body, mouth, hands,
I wait behind velvet, drawn in drunk by the chords and
    patterns and beats that cue dance.

III.

As am I, so are you, profoundly yoked to what sweeps and
    thunders above, around, within us,
You do not believe me, I see your face, I feel your doubt.
    I understand why so few dance.

IV.

He asked what was different about me, and I tried to
  speak my pulses, heartbeats, history,
He taunted, he jeered, ah, I know, I see, this is for men,
  this is what you do to woo, dance.

V.

Dheepa, it is no matter! You know this is passage between
  yourself and throbbing creation,
It is more than show, more than story, more than a human
  being on a stage, true dance.

Dheepa Maturi

Prompt: Dheepa Maturi writes a ghazal about dance, a mode
of expression with a deep personal meaning for her. Write a
ghazal about something to do with an art form, expressive
mode, or hobby that is close to your heart. That might be
dance, painting or drawing, writing, hiking, boating or soccer,
sewing, or even math or coding. Try to convey various meanings
the subject has for you, and how you connect to the history of
the practice.

Ghazal of the Lagoon

Morning, on the promenade, there's a break in the light
rain here in the serene republic. I take in the light.

Every walker gets lucky at this gaming table,
where the gondoliers, like croupiers, rake in the light.

through the glare of a restaurant's window, I see
fish glinting, like spear points that shake in the light.

I could sit on the edge and get wet forever,
all to consider a speed boat's wake in the light.

Furnaces burn. We sweat until we shine, fired up
by the wavy vases glassblowers make in the light.

Row me out, friars, in your *sandolo* on the waves
that glitter like ducats, for God's sake, in the light.

John Drury

Prompt: John Drury writes a ghazal about one place and time, where he seems to be a relaxed observer taking in the sparkling imagery of what's around him. Write a ghazal about a beautiful place and what is going on there, trying to give a sense of the overall feeling the place has through tiny, sparkling glimpses.

(Note: long-line poem below wraps to indents)

A Ghazal for the Diaspora

We have always been the displaced children of displaced
children,
Tethered by distant rivers to abandoned lands, our blood's
history lost.

To temper the grief, imagine your father's last breath as a
Moghul garden—
Marble pool at its centre, the mirrored sky holding all his
tribe had lost.

Above the tussle of his wounded city, sad-eyed paper kites
fight to stay aloft.
One lucky child will be crowned the winner, everyone else
will have lost.

Wish peace upon every stranger who arrives at your door,
even the thief—
For you never know when your last chance at redemption
will be lost.

In another version of the story, a steady loneliness mothers
away the rust.
Yet, without windows in its hull, the time-traveler's suppli-
cation gets lost.

Against flame-lipped testimonies of exile's erasures, the
    swinging of an axe.
Felled banyan trees populate your nightmares, new en-
    lightenments lost.

The rim of this porcelain cup is chipped, so sip with prac-
    ticed caution.
Even a trace of blood will copper the flavor, the respite of
    tea now lost.

Tell me, Faisal, with what new surrender can you evade
    deeper damnation?
Whatever it is, hack away, before your children, too, become
    the Lost.

Faisal Mohyuddin

Prompt: Faisal Mohyuddin writes about the loss of home, community, place, and possibility—and a continual grief because of it. This loss is magnified by the absence of the usual in-line rhymes. Write about a grief that is both personal and much larger than that, either historical or current. Balance the large scale of your subject with your personal experience, so the poem comes across as an even whole, where both parts inform and speak to one another.

Pantoums

(Note: long-line poem below wraps to indents)

Bouncing Between Beds with Song

"Let's go fly a kite, up to the highest height"

Mary Poppins

See the magnolia bursting
with what could be and the blue-grey
two-story shy beside it? There,
go in now, up the stairs and back too many years

into what could be, into the blue-grey
and stair-stepping into the long hallway of age,
go in now, staring full-face all the many years
that separate adult's bed from child's dream.

Two-stepping down the long hallway of age,
here where you cannot stand still—
between adult's bed and child's dream—
this is where you learned to fly.

There is a time you cannot stand still,
a time to leap from the blue-grey hall.
This is where your voice learned to fly
bursting from throat through song, through story,

each time leaping from the blue-grey hall,
"up, up into the atmosphere" of movies,
bursting from throat through song, through story,
"up, up where the air is clear," Mary Poppins humming.

"Up, Up"—the atmosphere expanding as you moved
into each new sphere, past flying the kite, past the kite itself,
"up, up, where the air is clear," beyond Mary Poppins.
     Humming
yourself into belief, away from the world below

into each new sphere, past flying the kite, past the kite itself,
into the more real sky, the universe itself, all that was waiting
of yourself. What you believed flew away from the world
     below
with loud singing past the rooftops and soot-filled chimneys

into the more real sky, the universe itself, all that was waiting.
Dashing down the long hallway, you bounce on one bed,
     then the other
with loud singing, past the rooftops and soot-filled chimneys,
past the Mary Poppins stories—childhood

dashed. Down the long hallway, past the beds, the other
self waits. There are always two stories. There
the blue-grey of what was. Over there,
what could be, every magnolia bursting.

Marjorie Maddox

Prompt: Poet Marjorie Maddox uses repetition of color and visions of a house (both inside and out) to create a story-like world in her pantoum. The cycling through of these repetitions creates a cumulative effect of growing loss, leading to sudden disorientation at the hard, lone word *dashed,* at the beginning of the last stanza. Write a pantoum that uses color and visions of a building (both inside and out) that has sentimental meaning for you, to create a growing sense of loss or irrevocable change.

Cumbria Pantoum

The blue soughs into grey.
In and out of fog the cow
Stands in the flecked greenness of the hill,
Her head shaking the mist away.

In and out of fog the cow
Forces the clouds lower than they were. She stands,
Her head shaking the mist away
In this place I have visited before.

Forcing the clouds lower than they were she stands
Closer than you are to me now
In this place I have visited in dreams,
Waking into a path balanced with stones.

Closer than you are to me now
The sheep dirty with dung and briars
Waking into a path balanced with stones,
The small birds nervous on the path ahead.

The sheep dirty with dung and briars,
Sometimes remembered images emerge.
The small birds nervous on the path ahead,
A certain dread pumps their chests with music.

Sometimes remembered images emerge
The answers in the blueness of the phrase
A certain dread pumping the chest with music,
Mystery clouds its edge.

The answers in the blueness of the phrase,
The blue soughs into grey.
Mystery clouds the edges,
Stands in the flecked greenness of the hill.

Jill Baumgaertner

Prompt: Write a pantoum about a mysterious place. Think about what words and images deserve to be repeated and interwoven as you carefully build a disquieting or unfathomable scene.

Breath-Sound While Meditating

The sea retracts its breath-sound,
gathering into itself the voice resisting.
Inhalation's held within each Om.
Mist piles up as clouds. Zeus wheezes.

Gathering into itself, the voice, resisting
sea's mouth, swallows noise. Undulating Oms
in the mist pile up in clouds. Zeus wheezes,
his cry an alarm and joyous and thin.

Sea's mouth swallows noise. Undulating Oms,
lungs sound their hunger for air. In exhalation
his cry—an alarm and joyous and thin.
The becoming full in the letting go. It rains.

Lungs sound their hunger for air. In exhalation
the emptying begins within, now without:
the becoming, full in the letting go. It rains
one-syllables. They rise to the surface, lullabies.

The emptying begins within, now without
the holding back. Om hums whole
one-syllables. They rise to the surface—lullabies
the sea retracts—its breath-sound.

Maureen E. Doallas

Prompt: How is a pantoum like a meditation? Doallas employs the form to emulate cycles of breath. Write your own pantoum that examines an action you take—think about those actions you repeat, weave, or cycle through, whether physically, emotionally, or both.

Oblique Eulogy II

What is death like, she asks,
as if she believes I know.
Like sleep, I venture, not waking?
She nods, dubious.

As if she believes I know,
my mother comes in a dream.
She nods, dubious.
Her eyebrows meet like Frida Kahlo's.

My mother comes in a dream,
bends to three striped kittens in my bed.
Her eyebrows meet like Frida Kahlo's—
I've never noticed this.

Bent over kittens in my bed
she fades into me, becomes me
and I hardly notice.
It's expected, unremarkable.

She fades, becomes me.
Fused, we resemble neither one.
Unremarkable, unexpected,
above my bed her face was young.

Fused, we resemble neither one.
In sleep, never waking,
above my bed her face was young.
What is death like, she asks.

Juditha Dowd

Prompt: Juditha Dowd's pantoum slowly fuses two people into one, as the poem works its oblique spell through repetition and shifting perspective. Write a pantoum in which a person or item you identify at the beginning of the poem morphs into another thing or person by the end. Use the repeating lines as part of the action of morphing.

Odes

Ode on the Death of a Favourite Cat Drowned in a Tub of Goldfishes

'Twas on a lofty vase's side,
Where China's gayest art had dyed
The azure flowers that blow;

Demurest of the tabby kind,
The pensive Selima, reclined,
Gazed on the lake below.

Her conscious tail her joy declared;
The fair round face, the snowy beard,
The velvet of her paws,
Her coat, that with the tortoise vies,
Her ears of jet, and emerald eyes,
She saw; and purred applause.

Still had she gazed; but 'midst the tide
Two angel forms were seen to glide,
The genii of the stream;
Their scaly armour's Tyrian hue
Through richest purple to the view
Betrayed a golden gleam.

The hapless nymph with wonder saw;
A whisker first and then a claw,
With many an ardent wish,
She stretched in vain to reach the prize.
What female heart can gold despise?
What cat's averse to fish?

Presumptuous maid! with looks intent
Again she stretch'd, again she bent,
Nor knew the gulf between.
(Malignant Fate sat by, and smiled)
The slippery verge her feet beguiled,

She tumbled headlong in.
Eight times emerging from the flood
She mewed to every watery god,
Some speedy aid to send.
No dolphin came, no Nereid stirred;
Nor cruel Tom, nor Susan heard;
A Favourite has no friend!

From hence, ye beauties, undeceived,
Know, one false step is ne'er retrieved,
And be with caution bold.
Not all that tempts your wandering eyes
And heedless hearts, is lawful prize;
Nor all that glisters, gold.

Thomas Gray

Prompt: While most odes are dedicated to people and objects, they can also commemorate events. The Greeks were fond of this, as was Thomas Gray, who wrote this ode on the event of his cat's untimely passing. Write an ode to your own event, but steer clear of the usual weddings, graduations, and birthdays in favor of something unexpected. Like Gray, trace the story in detail while also praising the moments with vivid, elevated language.

Mrs. Goldwasser

Shimmered like butterscotch; the sun
had nothing on her. She bangled
when she walked. No one
did not love her. She shone,
she glowed, she lit up any room,
her every gesture jewelry.
And O, when she called us by name
how we all performed!
Her string of little beads,
her pearls, her rough-cut
gemstones, diamonds, we hung
about her neck. And when
the future pressed her flat,
the world unclasped, and tarnished.

Ron Wallace

Prompt: Ron Wallace's "Mrs. Goldwasser" combines a barely-sonnet structure with what the poet calls a "mini-ode." Write your own combination poem that uses one of the forms we've explored in this book to construct an ode. Want extra credit? Make your subject a teacher.

homage to my hips

these hips are big hips
they need space to
move around in.
they don't fit into little
petty places. these hips
are free hips.
they don't like to be held back.
these hips have never been enslaved,
they go where they want to go
they do what they want to do.
these hips are mighty hips.
these hips are magic hips.
i have known them
to put a spell on a man and
spin him like a top!

Lucille Clifton

Prompt: Like Lucille Clifton, write an ode to one of your best traits or qualities. Don't be shy! (After all, you don't need to show it to anyone if you'd rather keep it as your little ode secret.) Use parallel structure and repetition (Clifton uses "hips" eight times) to help celebrate your awesomeness.

Ode on Solitude

Happy the man, whose wish and care
   A few paternal acres bound,
Content to breathe his native air,
               In his own ground.

Whose herds with milk, whose fields with bread,
   Whose flocks supply him with attire,
Whose trees in summer yield him shade,
               In winter fire.

Blest, who can unconcernedly find
   Hours, days, and years slide soft away,
In health of body, peace of mind,
               Quiet by day,

Sound sleep by night; study and ease,
   Together mixed; sweet recreation;
And innocence, which most does please,
               With meditation.

Thus let me live, unseen, unknown;
   Thus unlamented let me die;
Steal from the world, and not a stone
               Tell where I lie.

Alexander Pope

Prompt: Alexander Pope wrote this poem when he was twelve. Let's all take a moment to silently curse him. Now, write your own ode to an abstraction, and show that little poet who's boss! Note that although Pope writes to "solitude," he still includes concrete details in his poem to help us understand what solitude looks and feels like. In other words, write to an abstraction, but don't write abstractly.

Ode to 9th & O NW – Washington D.C.

You hundred-year-old
bastion of merriment
You crumbling icon
You hollow walls
& sacrosanct floors
You kitchen where rice was burned
& whiskey spilled
You wondrous accident
You ephemeral cacophony
You crumbled piece of adulthood
You first taste of adulthood
You made laughter omnipresent
Wrapped seven of us within your
walls, locked the door
& swallowed the key
You roommate shuffleboard
You millennial experiment
You eye of the gentrified storm

You still tryna be Duke Ellington
in a world full of yoga studios
Three years in your grasp
& we watched them turn
the Boys & Girls Club
into happy hour
It's something about how you sit
on the corner, at the intersection
of where I learned to tell someone
they made me feel like everything
& nothing all at once
How you made growing
up existential
How one can be lulled into nostalgia
by the clamor of an audacious love.

Clint Smith

Prompt: Clint Smith's ode captures the bittersweet experience
of remembering a childhood home surrounded by change.
Along the way, he uses a "catalog technique," repeating *You*
for several lines, then &, and eventually *How*. Sometimes the
repetitions build for several lines and then break, which helps
the lullaby-incantation sense (intrinsic to cataloging) to build
but not dull. Write an ode to a neighborhood from younger
days, exploring a range of images and emotions. Try out the
catalog technique as you go.

Rondeaux

We Wear the Mask

We wear the mask that grins and lies,
It hides our cheeks and shades our eyes,—
This debt we pay to human guile;
With torn and bleeding hearts we smile,
And mouth with myriad subtleties.

Why should the world be over-wise,
In counting all our tears and sighs?
Nay, let them only see us, while
    We wear the mask.

We smile, but, O great Christ, our cries
To thee from tortured souls arise.
We sing, but oh the clay is vile
Beneath our feet, and long the mile;
But let the world dream otherwise,
    We wear the mask!

Paul Laurence Dunbar

Prompt: Paul Laurence Dunbar uses a mask as an extended metaphor in this rondeau. (What might the metaphor "stand for"?—it's your job to investigate!) Write your own rondeau that introduces a metaphor in the refrain then goes on to explore it in depth.

Death of a Vermont Farm Woman

Is it time now to go away?
July is nearly over; hay
Fattens the barn, the herds are strong,
Our old fields prosper, these long
Green evenings will keep death at bay.

Last winter lingered; it was May
Before a flowering lilac spray
Barred cold for ever. I was wrong.
  Is it time now?

Six decades vanished in a day!
I bore four sons; one lived; they
Were all good men; three dying young
Was hard on us. I have looked long
For these hills to show me where peace lay…
  Is it time now?

Barbara Howes

Prompt: Barbara Howes employs a question as her refrain, which creates a lingering, vulnerable effect. Write your own rondeau that uses a question for the refrain.

Cirque

The clown is dead when last we found
a grave excuse to look around
and peer inside the shadowed door
upon the third and final floor
we listened but heard not a sound.

The house sits back upon the ground—
suspended, still, a merry-go-round
and no one goes there anymore
the clown is dead.

There's nothing left to tell of now
except perhaps the tale of how
we found him there, when we explored
but then again, we're pretty sure
that none would cry out, in the town—
the clown is dead.

Sara Barkat

Prompt: Sara Barkat uses the rondeau's roundabout nature to turn a simple image into something surreal. The off-kilter effect is heightened by non-parallel verb tenses. Try using a simple image in your refrain, that when repeated begins to feel surreal or unsettling. Test out different verb tense combinations to see what additional effect you might be able to achieve.

At Mile 37

At mile 37 red poppies do abide
near fields of what we think will soon be corn,
past horses pale, their hearts held close inside
thin skin. Today is not a day to mourn,
though if I say I am not sad, I lied.

You're gone. We rose and took it in our stride.
We pedaled hard and spied white poppies worn
from drought. Until we reached a red clump wide.
At mile 37.

Only then the red blooms promised for our ride,
sought at every pickup truck's loud horn
that blared at us for forty-two May miles,
to the right, beneath a black mailbox beside
the road we found red poppies newly born.
At mile 37.

Megan Willome

Prompt: In her rondeau "At Mile 37," poet Megan Willome recalls the poppy image from "In Flanders Fields" while creating her own world of memory and grief. Write a rondeau that takes a central image from any other poem in this book and use it to create a new world. Will it be Keats's bright star? Alvarez's lizards? Chang's KitchenAid? Enjoy the process of re-reading and enjoying the poems we've explored as you let your imagination circle.

When Was That Due?

I meant to do that yesterday—
distilling sense from disarray—
a ready version sure to please,
a distillation made with ease.

With words I'm sure to find my way.
My agony's sincerest play—
each line another way to pray.
I tell myself (to stay appeased):
I meant to do that—

I'm late again. What can I say?
I thought I had a few more days.
The ways of time are such a tease—
those chances that I didn't seize.
I lie to claim it's all okay:
I meant to do that!

Allison Joseph

Prompt: Allison Joseph uses the rondeau form to capture the cyclical nature of procrastination and ensuing frustration. Write a rondeau that employs humor to highlight a very real human experience.

Found Poetry

Three Found Poems

Comprised of words and phrases in
The Audubon Society Field Guide Series
and *The Peterson Field Guide Series*

Star Head

Look directly into the face.

Radiating in a wheel-like fashion,
the absent center
(that small, wind-bearing organ)

may be removed
so that the entire corolla
breaks open.

Exposed, its astronomical number
sings both day and night
at frequencies far above the human register

and rids the body
of poisonous spirits.
Many can be collected directly
into a killing jar or other container

without the use of a net.
Preserved, they will keep
indefinitely.

Habitat

It is impossible
to transplant time,

to dig up without injury
the full root system

bluish, delicate, forked,
neither male nor female.

Transverse candelabra
seen only with the aid
of a binocular microscope,

it spreads and speeds
faster than it dies.

Uncanny

The origin of adults
is shrouded in mystery.
Nothing is known
about what they first looked like

or the circumstances
that made their appearance possible.
Identification is complicated
by extreme variability.
Nomenclature is incredibly jumbled,
and species are juggled about
with capricious ease.
Many can change
their proportions
drastically, become
extremely contracted
or unnaturally distorted.
Sharply toothed, they may
be mistaken for ghosts,
but they break into pieces
at the slightest provocation,
so are best left alone.

Claire Batemen

Prompt: Write a poem, or series of poems (as above), found from a nonfiction reference source. You may worry that reference material, unlike fiction or poetry, won't sound "poetic" enough. However, when you select and juxtapose phrases and images from a discipline's specialized language, you can find many refreshing surprises.

Cento

When I have died, come find me
deep, quiet, and alone;
king of my beheaded kingdom
under a black lacquered moon.
The syllables of your name
disappear without memory
a small betrayal in the mind
in lapis, your gift to me.
It was darker then, in the nights
no lightning, no rain in weeks,
halfway from sleep to waking
I felt the winter in my veins.
We may miss our star
carved out of the night sky
almost alone because of lightning
to search for evidence of your existence.
Almost dreaming, nearly gone
we watched the sky descend—
light beacons standing in the cold
we were cracked against the sky.
On whom the pale moon gleams
we fashion an empire's glory
hidden in the sound of rain
the luminous emerald that pours over me
A hurricane's remnant
takes on its own unnatural blue
a swirl of colors in the distance
which is of course illusion.

In your silhouette I can still see myself
I glitter in the last light,
lying in the buried past
stars will fall and burn me.

Sara Barkat

Lines used from: "The Planet," Megan Fernandes; "A Ritual
to Read to Each Other," William Stafford; "The Ocean,"
Nathaniel Hawthorne; "Eclipse of My Third Life," Saeed
Jones; "Horse Sense," Richard Maxson; "How one winter
came in the lake region," William Wilfred Campbell; "Biolu-
minescence," Jeff Worley; "For Tony, and for the Morning,"
Robin Davidson; "Evening—before turning back the clock,"
Serena J. Fox; "An Appetite for Rain," Rebecca Lindenberg;
"Nostalgia," Dawn Potter; "Ode," Arthur O'Shaughnessy;
"Night Passage," Kathryn Neel; "The Orange Cat," Alicia Os-
triker; "Ghazal 838," Rumi; "Family Vacation," Jody
Zorgdrager; "Mars Poetica," Wyn Cooper; "Tattoo Thoughts,"
Dzvinia Orlowski; "Chimera," Jennifer Elise Foerster

Prompt: In this cento, Sara Barkat started by choosing several
lines and a basic focus/imagery, then she searched for poems
with similar lines. She continued by moving the lines around,
then finding and adding more until she came up with a satisfy-
ing flow. Write a cento of at least twenty lines, loosely organized around a basic focus or image, taking each line from a
different poem.

Skywoman, the trees, and fire

What the fire hears, red, willow and aster:
Fire, too, whispers, "I hear, I hear,"

and all the woods shiver, ravel,
unravel. A few survive.

Skywoman considers: Being, unbeing,
to the place where the day begins.

The voice is heard, over hands,
over asters, wanting or not wanting.

She longs to hear the whispers of fire,
what the willow hears: the foretelling,

how the mother, braiding sweetgrass,
hand over hand, weaves her story

day into night, the sound of silver bells,
silvery trill on the still-bare branches

shivers the air, draws her to the place
where the day begins, settles in her mind.

She asks if gratitude, too, is a citizen,
and braids gratitude in the hem of her skirt.

Gratitude becomes a story of wanting,

a wanting of story, and she feels the whispers

like sugar and bells. She braids sweetgrass
around her heart, soothed by songs.

Wanting the woods, she follows the sound
of searching, hand over hand.

Glynn Young

Prompt: Glynn Young wove this poem from tweets posted during a "Twitter Poetry Party," in which participants played off each other's words and quotes from *Braiding Sweetgrass: Indigenous Wisdom, Scientific Knowledge and the Teaching of Plants* by Native American botanist Robin Wall Kimmerer. Create your own found poem using the language of social media. You could either plan or participate in a collaborative event, as described above, or go through your Facebook, Twitter, or Instagram feed to select and weave together intriguing phrases.

Haiku

a deep gorge...
some of the silence
is me

John Stevenson

Prompt: John Stevenson writes a haiku where the poet appears in the poem, dwarfed by other imagery, making the poet seem to be part of the wider scene. The "deep gorge" and the silence of it become even more palpable. Write a haiku where your appearance is there to draw attention to and expand the subject of the poem.

clouds seen
through clouds
seen through

Jim Kacian

Prompt: Jim Kacian creates the feeling of movement or something continuous—without apparent end—through his use and re-use of the same words, strategically visually placed. Write a haiku where you repeat at least one phrase, strategically visually placed, so the repetition makes it feel endless.

wild iris—
the blazed trail stops
short of the meadow

Carolyn Hall

Prompt: Carolyn Hall writes a haiku about a flower that is brilliant and lively, and existing only because "the blazed trail" stopped. Write a poem about a beautiful, unexpected juxtaposition that could only exist because of its context.

bills paid
the tiger lily
past its prime

Roberta Beary

Prompt: Roberta Beary uses wordplay and puns to create a poem that's about both a tiger lily and an aging woman. Write a haiku with one image that could be taken either as a literal image or as a metaphor for something else. Use puns if you can! (Bashō would love you.)

distant thunder
the future
in my bones

Lorin Ford

Prompt: Lorin Ford uses sensory images other than the visual in her haiku, with the combination of "distant thunder" and "in my bones," creating a rumbling, tactile sensation. Write a haiku where the central image relies on one of the senses other than sight. (Smell, touch, taste, or sound.)

A Hallowe'en mask,
>   floating face up in the ditch,
>   slowly shakes its head.

Clement Hoyt

Prompt: In this haiku, Clement Hoyt creates an eerie, mini horror story by crafting a feeling of "life" or sentience where there shouldn't be (at least if you think from a non-Shintoism perspective!). This living sense in an inanimate object conspires to produce a foreboding feeling of being warned. Try your hand at a horror haiku. The image is key: think of the smallest moment/image you can come up with that could be uncanny or off.

Thirteen Ways of Looking at a Blackbird

I

Among twenty snowy mountains,
The only moving thing
Was the eye of the blackbird.

II

I was of three minds,
Like a tree
In which there are three blackbirds.

III

The blackbird whirled in the autumn winds.
It was a small part of the pantomime.

IV

A man and a woman
Are one.
A man and a woman and a blackbird
Are one.

V

I do not know which to prefer,
The beauty of inflections

Or the beauty of innuendoes,
The blackbird whistling
Or just after.

VI

Icicles filled the long window
With barbaric glass.
The shadow of the blackbird
Crossed it, to and fro.
The mood
Traced in the shadow
An indecipherable cause.

VII

O thin men of Haddam,
Why do you imagine golden birds?
Do you not see how the blackbird
Walks around the feet
Of the women about you?

VIII

I know noble accents
And lucid, inescapable rhythms;
But I know, too,
That the blackbird is involved
In what I know.

IX

When the blackbird flew out of sight,
It marked the edge
Of one of many circles.

X

At the sight of blackbirds
Flying in a green light,
Even the bawds of euphony
Would cry out sharply.

XI

He rode over Connecticut
In a glass coach.
Once, a fear pierced him,
In that he mistook
The shadow of his equipage
For blackbirds.

XII

The river is moving.
The blackbird must be flying.

XIII

It was evening all afternoon.

It was snowing
And it was going to snow.
The blackbird sat
In the cedar-limbs.

Wallace Stevens

Prompt: Wallace Stevens starts this poem sequence with haiku-inspired verse; then progresses to slightly longer, more introspective poems; and finally brings the meditation back to haiku-inspired verse at the end. Write a thirteen-poem sequence that is a mix of haiku (either strict or flexible) and free verse, all around one central image—natural or man-made; a moment or event; or a piece of figurative art, like a drawing, painting, or sculpture.

Plan Your Future Itinerary

You've just taken a guided tour of ten fabulous forms and variations, but the world of form is a very big place! If you get the urge to wander even further, you're invited to stop in to **TweetspeakPoetry.com** to explore more forms like...

Ballad

Catalog

Cinquain

Epic

Limerick

You can also find infographics for some of the form poems you've already met in this book:

Acrostic

Ghazal

Haiku

Ode

Pantoum

Rondeau

Sonnet (Quatrain Wreck!)

Tanka

For poet interviews regarding many of the poems in this volume and to hear recordings of the poets reading their poems, visit: **tweetspeakpoetry.com/category/poet-a-day/**

Enjoy your continued journey!

Notes

Epigraph

p. i   "Every day is a journey": Matsuo Bashō (Author), Nobuyuki Yuasa (Translator), *The Narrow Road to the Deep North and Other Travel Sketches* (New York: Penguin Classics, 1967), Kindle edition.

p. i   "Even the briefest form of poetry": Jane Hirshfield, *Ten Windows: How Great Poems Transform the World* (New York: Alfred A. Knopf, 2015), p. 88.

Opening Map

p. 17   "Forms are—as we believe—not locks, but keys": Mark Strand and Eavan Boland, eds, *The Making of a Poem: A Norton Anthology of Poetic Forms* (W.W. Norton & Company, 2000), p. xiii.

Chapter 1

p. 21   "The villanelle form has belonged almost entirely to English": Amanda French, *Refrain, Again: The Return of the Villanelle,* p. 7 (Amanda French website, accessed online May 2020). <http://amandafrench.net/villanelle>

Chapter 2

p. 40   "Cincinnati Walking Sonnet Project": Pauletta Hansel, "Cincinnati Walking Project" (*The Poet's Craft,* accessed online May 2020). <https://paulettahansel.wordpress.com/cincinnati-poet-laureate/cincinnati-walking-sonnet-project/>

Chapter 3

p. 50   "synchronicities and reverberations of life itself": Ben Yagoda, "Sestinapalooza" (*The Chronicle of Higher Education,* November 10, 2013, accessed online May 2020). <https://www.chronicle.com/blogs/linguafranca/sestinapalooza>

p. 54   "History" (North Point Lighthouse, Milwaukee, Wisconsin, accessed online Feb. 2020). <https://northpointlight house.org/learn/history>

p. 55   "...the path of a point in a plane moving": (*Merriam-Webster,* "spiral," accessed online May 2020). <https://www.merriam-webster.com/dictionary/spiral>

p. 62   "Since Wailing is a Bud of Causeful Sorrow": Sir Phillip Sydney, in Marianne Shapiro, ed., *Hieroglyph of Time: The Petrarchan Sestina* (Minneapolis: University of Minnesota Press, 1981, p. 178; Google Books, accessed online March 2021). <https://books.google.com/books?id= aaOAtcxHw2YC&pg>

Chapter 4

p. 65   ". . .many of these poems do not mention O'Hara's lover by name": Andrew Epstein, "Vincent Warren, Love of Frank O'Hara's Life, Passes Away at 79" (*Locus Solus: The New York School of Poets,* November 11, 2017, accessed online May 2020). <https://newyorkschoolpoets.wordpress.com/2017/ 11/11/vincent-warren-love-of-frank-oharas-life-passes-away-at-79/comment-page-1>

Chapter 5

p. 73   "...ceaselessly hungers for the absent beloved": Shadab Zeest Hashmi, *Ghazal Cosmopolitan: The Culture & Craft of the Ghazal* (Durham, NC: Jacar Press, 2017), p. viii.

p. 76   "The ghazal is made up of couplets, each autonomous": Agha Shahid Ali, *Ravishing Disunities: Real Ghazals in English* (Hanover, NH: Wesleyan University Press, 2000), p. 2.

p. 86   Ghazal meter: Feroz Khan, "Rules of Classical Poetry" (*Ferozghazal,* accessed online March 2021). < http://ferozg hazal.freeservers.com/catalog.html >

p. 86   Ghazal meter: Irfin 'Abid,' "Bah'r: The Backbone of
          Shaayari" (*Urdu Poetry Archive,* accessed online March 2021).
          < http://www.urdupoetry.com/articles/art5.html >

p. 86   Ghazal meter: Nimit, "Meter Of A Ghazal" (*Chaos in Brain,*
          accessed online March 2021). < https://chakarghinni.word
          press.com/2014/04/26/meter-of-a-ghazal/ >

p. 87   "many different behers used to write a ghazal": Frances W.
          Pritchett and Khaliq Ahmad Khaliq, *Urdu Meter: A Practical
          Handbook* (Columbia.edu, 1987, accessed online March 2021).
          <www.columbia.edu/itc/mealac/pritchett/00ghalib/
          meterbk/00_index.html>

Chapter 6

p. 88   ". . .the reader takes four steps forward, then two back":
          Eavan Boland and Mark Strand, *The Making of a Poem*
          (New York: W.W. Norton & Company, 2001), p. 44.

p. 88   "always looking back over its shoulder": Edward Hirsch,
          Poets' Glossary (New York: Houghton Mifflin Harcourt, 2014),
          p. 442.

p. 89   "known as a pantun berkait": Francois-Rene Daillie, *Alam
          Pantun Melayu: Studies on the Malay pantun* (Kuala Lumpur:
          Dewan Bahasa dan Pustaka, 1988), p. 38.

p. 97   "...poetic forms can bring an explorative freedom": Seth
          Haines, "Freedom in Structure: The Pantoum (A Writing
          Prompt)" (*Tweetspeak Poetry,* March 18, 2013, accessed online
          May 2020). <https://www.tweetspeakpoetry.com/2013/
          03/18/freedom-in-structure-the-pantoum-a-writing-
          prompt/>

p. 101   "Many pantuns are about good deeds": "Pantun: Indonesia
          and Malaysia" (UNESCO's Intangible Cultural Heritage,

2020, accessed online in March 2021). <https://ich.unesco.org/en/RL/pantun-01613>

p. 101   Pantun explanation: Vity, "Indonesian Pantun—Types—Examples" (*Mastering Bahasa,* April 2018, accessed online in March 2021). <https://masteringbahasa.com/indonesian-pantun>

p. 101   "'mime in classical ballet,' says Katherine Sim, as Cliff Goddard quotes in his study of active metaphors": Katherine Sim, in Cliff Goddard, "The ethnopragmatics and semantics of 'active' metaphors" (*Journal of Pragmatics,* accessed online February 2021). <http://nycklar.synthasite.com/resources/Goddard_Active_Metaphor.pdf>

p. 101   "A cane of sugar on a far-off shore": Anonymous pantun. Translated by L.L. Barkat.

Chapter 7

p. 111   Rondeau template: E.V. Wyler, "How to Write a Rondeau" (*The Society of Classical Poets,* October 5, 2016, accessed online May 2020). <https://classicalpoets.org/2016/10/05/how-to-write-a-rondeau-in-flanders-fields/>

p. 112   Robert Bridges triolet: E. Littell, ed., *The Living Age,* Seventh Series, Volume IV (Boston: The Living Age Company, 1899), p. 484 (Google Books accessed online March 2021). <https://books.google.com/books?id=k7IxAQAAMAAJ>

p. 113   "A rondelet": Charles Henry Luders, *The Literary World,* April 1889, in *The Magazine of Poetry: A Quarterly Review* (Buffalo, New York: Charles Wells Moulton, 1889), p. 382 (Google Books, accessed online March 2021). <https://books.google.com/books?id=3TxXAAAAMAAJ&pg=PA382&lpg=PA382&dq=rondelet>

Chapter 8

p. 118   "One of Horace's odes was also made to be sung, for a big event": R. J. Tarrant, "Lyricus Vates: Musical Settings of Horace's Odes" in *Reception and the Classics in Yale Classical Studies 36*, ed. William Brockliss, Pramit Chaudhuri, Ayelet Haimson Lushkov and Katherine Wasdin, 72-93 (Cambridge: Cambridge University Press) (Digital Access to Scholarship at Harvard accessed online in March 2021). <http://nrs.harvard.edu/urn-3:HUL.InstRepos:8919560>

p. 128   "two ways to go about converting a longum/brevis meter": Ben Glaser, "Polymetrical Dissonance: Tennyson, A. Mary F Robinson, and Classical Meter," p. 203-207 (Yale, accessed online March 2021). <english.yale.edu/sites/default/files/files/VP%20Essay%20Glaser.pdf>

p. 128   "Tennyson did in his self-aware poem 'Hendecasyllabics:'" Ibid, p. 202.

Chapter 9

p. 133   "Immature poets imitate; mature poets steal": T. S. Eliot in Philip Massinger, *The Sacred Wood: Essays On Poetry and Criticism by T. S. Eliot* (London: Methuen & Company Ltd., 1920), p. 114 (Internet Archive, accessed online March 2021). <https://quoteinvestigator.com/tag/t-s-eliot/#return-note-5574-2>

p. 133   "Code of Best Uses in Fair Use for Poetry": (*The Found Poetry Review*, accessed online May 2020). <http://www.foundpoetryreview.com/about-found-poetry/>

p. 139   "Happy poets who write found poetry go pawing through popular culture like": *Annie Dillard, Mornings Like This: Found Poems* (New York: Harper Perennial, 1996), Kindle edition.

p. 140   "images of peace and universality": Maayan Silver, "A Deeper

Look At Milwaukee's South Side 'Mural Of Peace'" (WUWM Milwaukee's NPR, accessed online May 2020). <https://www.wuwm.com/post/deeper-look-milwaukees-south-side-mural-peace#stream/0>

p. 141 "women who used to dye nylons there": Laura Kezman quoting a press release in "Who Decides What Becomes a Mural in Milwaukee" (Radio Milwaukee, Milwaukee, August 27th, 2019, accessed online May 2020). <https://radiomilwaukee.org/story/arts-culture/who-decides-what-becomes-a-mural-in-milwaukee/>

p. 142 "Notes from the Spectrum": Daniel Bowman, Jr., "Notes from the Spectrum" column (*Ruminate Magazine,* 2016, accessed online May 2020). <https://www.ruminatemagazine.com/search?type=article&q=notes+from+the+spectrum>

Chapter 10
p. 147 "If you have three or four, even five or seven extra syllables": Matsuo Bashō in Jane Hirshfield, *Ten Windows: How Great Poems Transform the World* (New York: Alfred A. Knopf, 2015), p. 82.

p. 148 "inviting, as Jane Hirshfield puts it, a 'renewed intensity of'": Jane Hirshfield, *Nine Gates: Entering the Mind of Poetry* (New York: Harper Perennial, 1997), p. 86.

p. 149 "…a eureka discovery for me [that] had nothing to do with syllable": Christopher Patchel, "Why Haiku: Not Just 5-7-5" (*Tweetspeak Poetry,* December 17, 2012, accessed online May 2020). <https://www.tweetspeakpoetry.com/2012/12/17/why-haiku-not-just-5-7-5/>

p. 152 "Haiku are a moment, a breath. If we're using travel as a metaphor": Joshua Gage, personal correspondence, January 26, 2020.

p. 156   "bring my mind to a place of calm": Rose Caiola, "Rewire Your Day with a Haiku Walk" (*Rewire Me,* April 2013, accessed online May 2020). <https://www.rewireme.com/ happiness/rewire-your-day-with-a-haiku-walk/>

p. 157   "the 'artless expression of a child at play'": Jane Hirshfield, *Ten Windows: How Great Poems Transform the World* (New York: Alfred A. Knopf, 2015), p. 91.

Switchbacks

p. 159   "form that either matches or purposely works against how you feel": L.L. Barkat, "Form It" column (*Tweetspeak Poetry,* accessed online May 2020). <https://www.tweetspeak poetry.com/category/form-it/>

Permissions

All poems in this book are reprinted with permission or are within the public domain. We are grateful to the authors, editors, and publishers who have given us permission to include these poems.

Anonymous, "A sugar cane…" The Malaysian version of this poem is in the public domain. Translation by L.L. Barkat, 2021. Reprinted with permission of the translator.

Janet Aalfs, "Ode to a Lost Sweater," from *Versewrights* #22, April 2015. Versewrights.com. Reprinted with permission of *Tweetspeak Versewrights*.

Matsuo Allard, "an icicle," from Cicada 3:2, 1979. No known literary executor.

Celia Lisset Alvarez, "Lizards," from *Poets and Artists: Oranges and Sardines* 3, no. 6, July 2010. Reprinted with permission of the author.

L.L. Barkat, "At the Window," May 7, 2009, author's blog. Reprinted with permission of the author.

L.L. Barkat, "The Proposal," from *The Novelist: A Novella,* T. S. Poetry Press, 2012. Reprinted with permission of the author.

Sara Barkat, "Cento," from *Every Day Poems,* 2020. Reprinted with permission of the author.

Sara Barkat, "Cirque," from *Every Day Poems,* 2016. Reprinted with permission of the author.

Matsuo Bashō, "Upon a lifeless branch…" The Japanese version of this poem is in the public domain. Translation by L.L. Barkat, 2021. Reprinted with permission of the translator.

Claire Bateman, "Three Found Poems" (originally published as "Star Head," "Habitat," and "Uncanny"), from *PoetryWTF,* February 2018. Reprinted with permission of the author.

Jill Baumgaertner, "Cumbria Pantoum," from *Ariel* VI, 1987. Reprinted with permission of the author.

Roberta Beary, "bills paid," from *The Unworn Necklace,* Snapshot Press, 2007. Reprinted with permission of the author.

Zeina Hashem Beck, "Ghazal: Back Home," from *Louder than Hearts,* Bauhan Publishing, 2017. Reprinted with permission of the author.

Elizabeth Bishop, "Sestina," from Poems. Copyright © 2011 by The

Aaron Brown, "Ghazal," from *Acacia Road,* Silverfish Review Press, 2016. Reprinted with permission of the author.

Barbara Crooker, "Crepuscule" (originally published as "Deer at Twilight"), from *The MacGuffin,* 2020. Reprinted with permission of the author.

Charles B. Dickson, "dense fog," *Appalachian Twilight,* HC Sheet, 1987. No known literary executor.

Maureen E. Doallas, "Breath-Sound While Meditating," 2013. Reprinted with permission of the author.

Juditha Dowd, "Oblique Eulogy II," from *What Remains,* Finishing Line Press, 2009. Reprinted with permission of the author.

Paul Laurence Dunbar, "We Wear the Mask," 1895. This poem is in the public domain.

John Drury, "Ghazal of the Lagoon," from *The Disappearing Town,* Miami University Press, 2000. Reprinted with permission of the author.

deb y felio, "asking me to pause," 2018. Reprinted with permission of the author.

Lorin Ford, "distant thunder," from The Haiku Foundation (thehaikufoundation.org), 2010. Reprinted with permission of the author.

Joshua Gage, "coffee break," from *Frogpond* 41:2, Summer 2018. Reprinted with permission of the author.

Joshua Gage, "Super bowl" and "melting snow," 2020. Reprinted with permission of the author.

Joshua Gage, "In the Summer," *from a branch of coral flame* (Thesis: MA in English), Cleveland State University, 2004. Reprinted with permission of the author.

Albert Giraud, "Lune Au Lavoir," 1912. The French version of this poem is in the public domain. "Lady Moon Launders" translation by L.L. Barkat, 2021. Reprinted with permission of the translator.

Thomas Gray, "Ode on the Death of a Favourite Cat Drowned in a
    Tub of Goldfishes," 1748. This poem is in the public domain.

Seth Haines, "November Pyres," from Tweetspeakpoetry.com, 2013.
    Reprinted with permission of the author.

Carolyn Hall, "wild iris," from *Modern Haiku*, XXXIV:3, Autumn
    2003. Reprinted with permission of the author.

Clement Hoyt, "A Hallowe'en mask," *AH* 1:2, 1963. No known
    literary executor.

Barbara Howes, "Death of a Vermont Farm Woman" from
    The Collected Poems of Barbara Howes. Copyright © 1995 by Barbara
    Howes. Reproduced with the permission of the University of
    Arkansas Press, www.uapress.com.

Tom Hunley, "It's Not So Hard to Write a Sonnet, Man," from
    Valparaiso Poetry Review, Fall/Winter 2018-2019. Reprinted with
    permission of the author.

Marci Rae Johnson, "#DoDifferentDaily," 2020. Reprinted with
    permission of the author.

Ashley M. Jones, "Harriette Winslow and Aunt Rachel Clean Collard
    Greens on Prime Time Television," *from dark//thing,* Pleiades Press,
    2019. Reprinted with permission of the author.

Ashley M. Jones, "Kindergarten Villanelle," from *dark//thing,*
    Pleiades Press, 2019. Reprinted with permission of the author.

Allison Joseph, "When Was That Due?" 2020. Reprinted with
    permission of the author.

Erin Keane, "Science Fiction," from *The Gravity Soundtrack,*
    WordFarm, 2007. Reprinted with permission of the publisher.

John Keats, "Bright star, would I were stedfast as thou art—," 1819.
    This poem is in the public domain.

John Keats, "To Autumn," 1820. This poem is in the public domain.

Jim Kacian, "clouds seen," from *The Haiku Anthology,* W.W. Norton,
    1999. Reprinted with permission of the author.

Sandra Heska King, "To My Mother," 2011. Reprinted with permission
    of the author.

Rebecca Lauren, "Ode to Butter," 2020. Reprinted with permission
    of the author.

Chip Livingston, "Punta del Este Pantoum," from *SING: Poetry of the*

Indigenous Americas, University of Arizona Press, 2011. Reprinted with permission of the author.

Amy Lowell, "Nuance," from *Pictures of the Floating World,* Houghton Mifflin, 1919. This poem is in the public domain.

Marjorie Maddox, "Bouncing Between Beds with Song," from *SWWIM,* October 2017. Reprinted with permission of the author.

Katie Manning, "The Book of Class," from *Ryga,* 2019. Reprinted with permission of the author.

Katie Manning, "Time Falling," 2020. Reprinted with permission of the author.

Dheepa Maturi, "The Ancient Dance: A Ghazal," from *Every Day Poems,* 2016. Reprinted with permission of the author.

Richard Maxson, "Please Stay," 2019. Reprinted with permission of the author.

Richard Maxson, "The Sirens," from *Every Day Poems,* 2019. Reprinted with permission of the author.

John McCrae, "In Flanders Fields," 1915. This poem is in the public domain.

Claude McKay, "I Shall Return," 1920. This poem is in the public domain.

Faisal Mohyuddin, "A Ghazal for the Diaspora," from *The Displaced Children of Displaced Children,* Eyewear Publishing, 2018. Reprinted with permission of the author.

Faisal Mohyuddin, "To Be a Fisherman, Or a Father, You Must," from *The Displaced Children of Displaced Children,* Eyewear Publishing, 2018. Reprinted with permission of the author.

Benjamin Myers, "The Muse," from *Rock & Sling,* 2012. Reprinted with permission of the author.

Michelle Ortega, "Let the Questions Go Unanswered," *Contemporary Haibun Online,* Vol. 15 No. 3, October 2019. Reprinted with permission of the author.

Angela Alaimo O'Donnell, "Notebook Cento," 2020. Reprinted with permission of the author.

Conor O'Callaghan, "Three Six Five Zero," from *The Sun King,* 2013. Reprinted with permission of the author and The Gallery Press, Loughcrew, Oldcastle, County Meath, Ireland.

Elise Paschen, "The Front Room," from *Houses: Coasts,* Sycamore Press, 1985. Reprinted with permission of the author.

Christopher Patchel, three haiku from *Turn Turn,* Red Moon Press, 2013. Reprinted with permission of the author.

Richard Pierce, "Go Gentle," from *Image Journal,* Fall 2016. Reprinted with permission of the author.

John Poch, "Echo," from *Fix Quiet,* St. Augustine's Press, 2015. Reprinted with permission of the author.

Edgar Allan Poe, "A Valentine," 1841. This poem is in the public domain.

Alexander Pope, "Ode on Solitude," 1700. This poem is in the public domain.

Ezra Pound, "In a Station of the Metro," 1913. This poem is in the public domain.

Susan Rothbard, "That New," from *Birds of New Jersey,* Broadkill River Press, 2021. Reprinted with permission of the author.

William Shakespeare, "Sonnet 116," 1609. This poem is in the public domain.

William Shakespeare, "Sonnet 130," 1609. This poem is in the public domain.

Monica Sharman, "What It Feels Like," 2012. Reprinted with permission of the author.

Murray Silverstein, "Sestina to Bind a Goodbye," from *Any Old Wolf,* Sixteen Rivers Press, 2006. Reprinted with permission of the author.

Clint Smith, "Ode to 9th and O NW–Washington D.C.," from Drunk in a Midnight Choir, https://drunkinamidnightchoir.word-press.com/2015/05/14/three-poems-clint-smith/, 2015. Reprinted with permission of the author.

Gabriel Spera, "Sonnet (With Children)," from *The Rigid Body,* Ashland Poetry Press, 2012. Reprinted with permission of the author.

Wallace Stevens, "Thirteen Ways of Looking at a Blackbird," *Others: An Anthology of the New Verse,* Alfred A. Knopf, 1917. This poem is in the public domain.

John Stevenson, "a deep gorge," from *Geppo,* July/August 1996. Reprinted with permission of the author.

Natasha Trethewey, "Incident," from *Native Guard,* Mariner Books,

2007. Reprinted with permission of the publisher and author.

Todd C. Truffin, "Summer Conditioning," 2016. Reprinted with permission of the author.

Jeanne Murray Walker, "The Creation," from *The Southern Review,* Autumn 2013. Reprinted with permission of the author.

Ron Wallace, "Mrs. Goldwasser" from the poem cycle entitled "Teachers: A Primer" from *Long for This World: New and Selected Poems,* 2003. Reprinted by permission of the University of Pittsburgh Press.

David K. Wheeler, "Lullaby for the Sunshine Silver Mine," from *Contingency Plans,* T. S. Poetry Press, 2010. Reprinted with permission of the publisher.

Isaac Willis, "A Sonnet for the Architect," from *The Cresset,* 2018. Reprinted with permission of the author.

Megan Willome, "At Mile 37," from *The Joy of Poetry: How to Keep, Save & Make Your Life With Poems,* T. S. Poetry Press, 2016. Reprinted with permission of the author.

David Wright, "When the Eye and the Ear and the Voice," appearing as part of "Sonnets to Accompany Bruch's Kol Nidrei" from *Crab Orchard Review,* Spring 2019. Reprinted with permission of the author.

Glynn Young, "Skywoman, the trees, and fire," from Tweetspeak poetry.com, 2019. Reprinted with permission of *Tweetspeak Poetry.*

Also from T. S. Poetry Press

How to Read a Poem: Based on the Billy Collins Poem "Introduction to Poetry," by Tania Runyan

"Runyan's book reads like a playful love letter—a creative intercession on poetry's behalf—to the hearts of a new generation, those on whom so much, like the future of the art, depends."

—Brad Davis, poet, teacher, and counselor at Pomfret School

The Yellow Wall-paper: A Graphic Novel—full text by Charlotte Perkins Gilman, 1892; Illustrations by Sara Barkat, 2020

"The mark of a good illustrator is one who somehow helps you see more than is in the words themselves and also somehow helps you to see more in your own mind than is on the page—Sara Barkat is that kind of illustrator."

—Megan Willome, author of *The Joy of Poetry*

Rumors of Water: Thoughts on Creativity & Writing, by L.L. Barkat (Twice named a Best Book of 2011)

"A few brave writers pull back the curtain to show us their creative process. Annie Dillard did this. So did Hemingway. Now L.L. Barkat has given us a thoroughly modern analysis of writing. Practical, yes, but also a gentle uncovering of the art of being a writer."

—Gordon Atkinson, Editor at Foundations for Laity Renewal

The Field Guide Series tutors on a practical level—
in matters of reading, writing, or the development
of writing careers.

T. S. Poetry Press titles are available online in e-book
and print editions.
Print editions also available through Ingram.

tspoetry.com

Made in the USA
Las Vegas, NV
03 August 2024

93310605R00146